The authors

Joy Claxton considers herself privileged to have learned her harness work over many years as a groom working under distinguished coachmen who had learned their skills at the turn of the century. Now retired from being a groom, the author is an animal portraitist and gains great pleasure from teaching disabled people to drive. Joy Claxton specialises in giving a good basic knowledge of driving to all who come to her.

Vivian Ellis started driving at seven with a family pony and at twelve was working with Shires and Percherons on local farms in her spare time. In 1968 the author founded a donkey stud and is currently a Donkey Breed Society Judge. In 1974 Vivian Ellis, together with the late Nancy Pethick, started to teach driving to disabled people. Mrs. Ellis is also a British Driving Society Judge, a member of the Tandem Club and has taught carriage driving since 1971.

Richard Ellis started driving at fifteen as a milk roundsman, worked with Suffolk Punches and Shires at college and farmed for 30 years with Irish Cobs. The author is a British Driving Society Council member, Chairman of the Area Commission Committee, a member of the Judges' Selection Committee, a Light Harness Horse Instructor and Verifier, a founder member of the Tandem Driving Club, and a member of numerous other driving committees. In addition, Richard Ellis is a teacher and lecturer.

Richard and Vivian Ellis own three horses and two ponies all of whom are driven as singles, pairs and tandems.

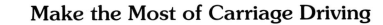

Make the Most of Carriage Driving

Make the Most of Carriage Driving

Vivian and Richard Ellis
and Joy Claxton

J.A. Allen
London

British Library Cataloguing in Publication Data
A catalogue record for this book is available from the British Library

ISBN 0. 85131. 602. 6

Published in Great Britain in 1995 by
J.A. Allen & Company Limited
1 Lower Grosvenor Place,
Buckingham Palace Road,
London, SW1W 0EL.

Designed by Nancy Lawrence

Typeset in Great Britain by Textype Typesetters
Printed and bound by Dah Hua Printing Press Co., Ltd,
Hong Kong

Contents

Foreword   Page   xi
Preface   xiii
Acknowledgements   xiv

1 An Introduction to Driving Activities   1

The History of Driving Clubs   1
Non-competitive Driving   2
    Rallies; Weddings; Fetes; Picnics; Shopping
Competitive Driving   5
    Long Distance Driving; Combined Driving;
    Scurry Driving
Driving for Disabled People   8

2 Choosing the Driving Animal   10

Size   11
Purchase for Specific Uses   12
Cost   12
Driving Donkeys   12
Temperament   13
Conformation and Movement   18

3 Care of the Driving Animal   23

Achieving Fitness   23
    Basic Signs of Fitness and Unfitness; The Coat
Principles of Feeding   25

4 Training the Animal to go in Harness   27
   Professional Schooling   27
   Training at Home   28
      The Blinkered Bridle and Driving Bit; Long-
      reining; Collar and Traces; Pulling a Tyre,
      Log or Harrow; Putting To for the First Time;
      Moving Off; Driving from the Vehicle

5 Dress and Equipment   34
   Dress   35
      Knee Rugs and Driving Aprons
   Driving Whips   35
      Types of Whip; Choice of Whip; Care of
      the Whip
   Spares   37

6 The Groom   40

7 Choice of Vehicle   42
   Features of a Good Vehicle   44
      Balance; The Shafts; Wheels; The Body;
      Special Features
   Naming Types of Vehicle   51

Vehicle Types: Advantages and Disadvantages   53
   Cranked Axles; Cab-fronted Vehicles;
   Pneumatic Tyres; Four- and Two-wheelers

8 Choice of Harness   54
   General Considerations   54
   Collars   60
      Checking the Fit of the Collar

9 Single Harness: Fitting and Putting To   65
   Fitting Single Harness   65
      The Collar; The Pad or Saddle, Back Band
      and Tugs; Back Strap and Crupper; The
      Breeching; The Reins; The Bridle
   Preparing to Put To   76
   Putting To   76
      Checking Balance of a Two-wheeled Vehicle
   Taking Out   78
      Unharnessing
   Variations in Harness and Harnessing   79
      Four-wheeled Vehicles with Independent
      Shafts; Harness for Donkeys and Mules;
      Bearing Reins ('Top' or 'Overcheck' Reins)

10 How to Drive in Single Harness   82

Changes in Technique   82
Preparing to Drive   83
   Mounting the Vehicle; Dismounting
The Art of Driving   85
   The Use of the Hands; Shortening the Reins;
   Emergency Stops; The Voice; The Whip
Off-vehicle Practise   89

11 Driving Pairs   93

Pairs Harness   94
   Harnessing Up; Putting To; Taking Out
Driving Pairs   100
   Dealing with Problems
Examples of Pairs Vehicles   103
   The Curricle; The Cape Harness or Cape
   Curricle

12 Driving Tandem   110

Tandem Vehicles   113
Tandem Harness   113
   Harnessing in Tandem; Putting To
Tandem Driving Techniques   119
   The English Method; The Hungarian or FEI
   Method; What Can Go Wrong

13 Driving a Team   124

Carriage Choice for Teams of Four   125
Harness for Teams   125
   Harnessing a Team
Driving a Four-in-hand   126

14 The Show Ring   130

Spectating   130
   The Park Drag; The Road Coach;
   Watching a Trade Class; Private Driving
   Classes; What the Show Judge Looks For
Show Ring Technique   139
   Procedure in the Collecting Ring;
   Entering the Ring; Show Ring Manners;
   Changing the Rein; The First Line-up;
   The Individual Display; The Final Line-up;
   Propriety
Dress for the Show Ring   144
   The Whip and Passengers; The Groom
Plaiting   148

15 Transportation   152

Transporting Driving Animals   152
Transporting Driving Vehicles   154

16 Vehicle Maintenance   156

Safety   156
   Wheels and Axles; Shafts; Floor
Performance   160
   Tyres; Brakes; Leaf Springs
Appearance   161

17 Harness Maintenance   162

18 Avoiding Accidents   164

The Highway Code   164
Consideration for Others   165
Correct Driving Practice   165
First Aid   167

19 Additional Animals   169

The Goat in Harness   169
The Coaching Dog – The Dalmatian   171

Index   173

Foreword

There are many books on driving, some of which are overelaborate. *Make the Most of Carriage Driving* is simple to understand, concise, and the advice given to readers is eminently practical.

The authors show the many ways in which horses, donkeys and goats may be driven, and their advice ranges from the elementary to tandem and team driving. Above all, the text is clear, sound in its advice, and even encompasses the training of a quadriga of donkeys for those who are looking for a new challenge.

One must also smile at the old adage quoted 'that a good driving animal should have the head of a duchess and the backside of a pastry cook' which only goes to prove that our forebears had a twinkling sense of humour.

I like the fact that the accepted way of doing things is sometimes questioned. To plait or not to plait? Well, I will let you make up your own mind when you have considered the advice given.

You certainly won't be bored by this book which is full of information.

John Richards
Chairman of the Carriage Foundation
and former Chairman of the BDS.

Preface

The English language is enriched with sayings from our coaching past.

When someone revolts against authority, they are said to have 'kicked over the traces', and their supervisor might consider them 'a bit of a handful' – an expression derived from the full hand method of driving a four-in-hand.

Calling someone an 'outsider' had its origin in the days when a person of different or lower social status could not afford a more expensive seat inside the coach, and therefore sat outside on the roof. Indeed, before coaches were fitted with proper roof seats, passengers travelling outside might literally 'drop off' if they fell asleep.

Before 'dropping off', a passenger might have been having a nightmare or, at least, a nightmare journey. This term, too, derives from coaching. Unscrupulous coach proprietors used to keep their worst horses and harness for the country stages of journeys, where all discomforts and disruptions could be blamed on the unmade tracks, and they used to keep their *very* worst and worn out animals – their 'night mares' for night time journeys on such tracks.

One coaching jobmaster actually got his own name into the English language. He always worked his horses in strict rotation, and his customers had to take what they were offered, or nothing at all. His name was Hobson, and his 'take it or leave it' approach became known as 'Hobson's choice'.

This book has been written to show that carriage driving need not be a matter of Hobson's choice. There are many types of animal who can be driven in harness; there is a wide choice of vehicles and formations, and there are all sorts of driving activities, competitive and non-competitive, to enjoy. So make the most of carriage driving.

Acknowledgements

The authors are grateful to Jennie Bourne and Sara Handley for their care and patience in preparing the typescript, and to Martin Diggle for editing the typescript.

CHAPTER 1

An Introduction to Driving Activities

Until well into the present century, horse-drawn vehicles in various forms provided the main means of transport for most people, goods and purposes. It is not surprising, therefore, that the driving enthusiast has inherited a wealth of activities to pursue, be they for pleasure, competition or a combination of the two.

The History of Driving Clubs

Although, historically, most carriage driving was a matter of necessity, there have always been sporting and recreational elements. Indeed, the first driving clubs were founded in the early years of the nineteenth century – although they were rather different from the clubs of today, being more like diners' clubs with members wearing outrageous fashions. Meeting once or twice a month in London, they drove out to the country to dine, returning home in the night.

The members of these clubs acquired rather dubious reputations through their behaviour and their dress. When the Richmond Driving Club started in 1838, the founders insisted that members drove like coachmen but looked like gentlemen. These clubs had rather short lives, the Crimean War striking the final blow to them.

After this War, however, the Four-in-Hand Club was founded; The Duke of Beaufort was its patron and his family colours were used for the club. They met in Hyde Park, and membership was limited to thirty.

The art of four-in-hand driving became so popular that the breakaway Coaching Club was started in June 1871. This club still exists and its members drive and dine together at least once a year. Their Park Drags make a wonderful sight.

After the 1914–18 War, when cars were becoming the usual means of transport, amateur Whips (drivers) formed themselves into clubs to keep alive the romance of the road and preserve the skills of tandem and four-in-hand driving. A few of them lasted up until the outbreak of the next War in 1939. In the aftermath, there was little money or enthusiasm for driving. People were increasingly keen to own cars and get from place to place as quickly as they could.

However, in 1952, Her Royal Highness The Princess Elizabeth wished for a horse-drawn coronation procession. The members of the Coaching Club helped to swell the ranks of this by horsing the Commonwealth Prime Ministers' carriages.

Out of this event grew the British Driving Society (BDS) which was actually formed in 1957. The aim of the BDS is to assist all those interested in driving horses and ponies. This society keeps judging and showing standards high, and has a series of proficiency tests which currently rate as recognised teaching qualifications, as well as a City and Guilds qualification for carriage grooms.

For administrative purposes the BDS divides the country into areas, each area having a commissioner who arranges for members to meet socially as well as to drive together in non-competitive rallies.

The BDS runs and administers the long distance driving competitions whilst the British Horse Society (BHS) does the same for cross-country driving and scurry competitions. Since not everyone can participate in these exacting activities there are strong supporters clubs associated with them.

There are also many local driving clubs throughout the country. Most of these clubs are affiliated to the BDS and can be contacted through it. Some are geared towards pleasure driving and others toward more competitive activities. Let us take a look at the range of activities they promote, and at some other activities which are available in the world of carriage driving.

Non-competitive Driving

This is probably the more popular form; at the time of writing the BDS has a membership in excess of 5,000. Many families have a pony who has been outgrown by the children and, rather than part with him, he is trained to harness, a vehicle and harness are purchased, the owners (usually the parents) learn to drive and at this point they find that, as well as shopping and visiting the pub or going for family picnics, they can go to rallies or one of the other non-competitive events and meet other people who have the same interests.

This is where the BDS plays such an important role. It publishes quarterly newsletters with lists of individual area activities, such as rallies or demonstration drives, often at village fetes or local shows. In this way there is a regular meeting of families with a common interest, and a great deal of fun is obtained from these drives.

Rallies

Summer rallies usually start at about 2–2.30 p.m. with a 'meet' in a field. Some members who live locally may drive their animals to the meet, others who live some distance away will box up and park in the field, where they unbox and harness up. When everybody is ready, the drive starts. It is usually led by whoever is hosting the meet, but it should always be led by an experienced, considerate person who knows the route and is able to set a steady, safe speed and will be aware of the needs and problems that may arise among those following.

An average rally is between 13 and 26 km (8 and 16 miles), with a stop halfway of about twenty minutes. This is, in theory, to give the animals a rest, but is often a chance for the humans to have a glass of cider, wine or a fruit juice, which is usually brought down the line by a steward of the drive. At this point, it is perhaps prudent to say that the average acceptable speed of the drive is 9.6–13 kph (6–8 mph). It is still an offence to drive an equine in excess of 19.3 kph (12 mph) and one can still be prosecuted for doing so!

After the halfway rest, the journey is completed and usually, on return to the field, the animals are taken out of their vehicles, unharnessed and rugged up – often after a quick spray with water from a carrier. They are then loaded into their boxes, tied up safely and provided with haynets, while their happy and exhausted owners go into the home of the host for a cup of tea, some light refreshment and a good gossip. In due course, everyone returns to their boxes, loads up their vehicles and goes home.

This form of driving is ideal for a family. It can be done with a single animal, or a pair, the latter of course to a four-wheeled vehicle, which is usually capable of carrying a family of four. Some brave people do attend rallies with tandems, but they are in the minority.

In the winter months rallies usually start at about 11.30 a.m. and, instead of tea on return to the hosts, a stand-up light fork lunch is given. This way everyone gets home mid-afternoon, which is an advantage in the winter.

Treasure hunts are another form of fun driving, as is sending people off at short intervals with a map. This can be a good change from the follow-my-leader effect of the traditional rally.

Weddings

Horse-drawn carriages are a lovely, traditional way of getting to and from a wedding and more and more horse and pony owners are venturing into this field. Sadly, in some cases, the standard of turnout and the safety factors are rather dismal.

Well schooled, obedient animals are necessary. The unexpected will cause an accident very quickly but, while accidents will and do happen, the risk can be reduced with hard work and knowledge. An accident is especially unwelcome on the occasion of a wedding. Harness must be regularly checked for wear, repaired and kept clean and supple. Vehicles must be carefully maintained, horses must be kept exercised, groomed and well shod. The Whip must keep his or her clothes clean and in good repair. Insurance for accidents and hire and reward must be kept up to date.

Transport, whether horsebox or trailer, must also be kept well maintained. Reliability is a very important aspect for the suppliers of carriages of horse-drawn weddings, as is punctuality and care with paperwork. Double-booking can easily be done, but this not only causes unhappiness to the brides and their families; it is also very embarrassing and gives a very bad impression of the horse world.

Fetes

Sometimes local village fetes ask the driving club members in their area to give a driving demonstration to the general public. For such events it is important that the animals used are sensible, used to driving in company with other turnouts, don't mind noise and general commotion from people, loudspeakers and music and, if there is a clay pigeon shoot at the fete, they must not take off when the guns are fired.

Training an animal to get used to music can easily be done by placing a radio inside or just outside the stable, choosing a programme with loud music and plenty of talking. Tapes with bagpipe music can also be a helpful addition, so that if there is a pipe band at the event, your animal will not be upset.

If there are a number of turnouts taking part at a fete demonstration, a very good impression can be given to the public by doing a musical drive. Following a good forward-going leader, circles, figures of eight, and changes of speed performed to music can give a very interesting and pleasurable effect which the general public usually enjoy greatly.

Again, it is most important that you are fully insured.

Picnics

A family picnic with one's horse, pony or donkey can be the greatest fun for everyone, but do remember two rather important things. First, when stopping for the picnic, make sure that the animal is held when unloading the picnic paraphernalia, or take him out of the vehicle and tie him to something strong, making sure he cannot eat any poisonous plants or cause any damage. Second, make sure that none of the children feed him anything with meat in it. Meat is very poisonous to all equines and, on a picnic, the animals do like to join in. One of our ponies has a great liking for cucumber sandwiches, so when taking her on a picnic we always tend to put one or two in specially for her.

Shopping

It is still possible to go shopping with pony and trap in rural areas. If an order is phoned through to the village store the day before, or a few hours ahead of when you are going out exercising, the goods can usually be put in a box and brought out to you in your vehicle. If you live in a very quiet, remote area, the owner of the local store will often be quite happy to have a tie ring on a wall by his shop. Then, if your animal is well trained and peaceful, you can pop a headcollar and leadrope over his bridle and tie him up while you shop. In the old days, everyone living in the country did this. Nowadays there are people who would throw their hands up in horror, saying you must never tie up an animal with his bridle still on. Again, it is a matter of training at home and using one's common sense when deciding whether it is a safe thing to do in your own particular circumstances.

A final reminder for this section on non-competitive activities: do remember to make sure in the summer months that your animal is protected from flies. There are many sprays and lotions on the market and it only takes a few seconds to spray or sponge on fly deterrent. This can prevent an accident– flies and wasps are a great nuisance and their bites and stings often cause the best-behaved animals to bolt.

Competitive Driving

This includes showing, long distance driving, combined driving (under FEI rules) and scurry.

Successful show driving requires considerable time, money, skill and practise. It is, however, the most accessible of the competitive driving sports, and a later chapter is devoted to it. The other sports place great demands upon the experience and skills of both Whip and back-up team; if these are not met in respect of technique, vehicle maintenance and horsemastership, then the safety and welfare of both humans and animals will be at risk. This is not to say, of course, that driving enthusiasts should not embrace these sports in time, but simply that they should be approached in due season. Since the primary concern of this book is to provide an introduction to driving, these sports are not addressed in the same detail as showing. However, the following synopses may be of interest both to those who aspire to future participation and to interested spectators.

Long Distance Driving

Long distance driving is a relatively new but fast-expanding sport. The BDS has encouraged this activity and, to ensure that the welfare of participating animals does not suffer through human ignorance, a committee with a vet as its chairman has been set up to ensure correct procedures and issue guidelines.

These are under constant review and, when considering whether to take part in a long distance drive, it would be sensible to contact the secretary of the BDS, who will always give the name of the current long distance committee chairman.

Like long distance riding, the driving is an interesting and exhilarating exercise, which requires a hard, fit, enthusiastic animal who does not get over-excited when asked to tackle all sorts of different terrain under varying conditions. Before commencing a long distance drive all animals have their pulse and breathing rates taken and recorded, as each animal has a slightly different rate. There are fixed stopping places, with set times for rest. The animals are checked for pulse rate etc. on arrival at these points and the time it takes for them to return to average natural rates is monitored. An interesting point to remember is that in the old days – in fact, until well into the twentieth century – farmers, doctors and other drivers still used horse-drawn transport for their everyday business life and their animals often had to be driven over 50 km (30 miles) a day – a great deal of which was track and hill work. The Cobs,

Dales, Fells and 'Vanners' were the most commonly used breeds and, with the right feeding and schooling, their lives were usually good and long. These days, their daily work distances would certainly be classed as 'long distance driving'.

Combined Driving

This sport, sometimes called 'FEI' after the governing body, calls for three major different skills in the art of rein handling, as well as postural differences of the Whip. The disciplines involved are:

Dressage. Here elegance, accuracy of movement within the arena and driving technique are the main criteria. The Whip should always be sitting with a straight back and sloping thighs. Traditionally, the reins were held in the left hand; the right hand controlling the whip and assisting the left hand. Nowadays, however, they can be held as when riding. Dress for the Whip is usually similar to that used for private driving classes in the show ring.

Marathon. Here accuracy of positioning both animals and vehicle safely at speed becomes the important factor. To do this, it is often necessary to lose the elegant style of dressage – to lean forwards on the pelvis, straddle the legs, use a rein in each hand and increase the decibel level of the voice for commands and encouragement to both animals and the grooms on the back of the vehicle. The masters of FEI are a pleasure to watch; the best of them manage to keep a great degree of elegance when tackling some of the rather difficult hazards that course builders like to produce. Dress is comfortable wear, though usually all persons in an individual turnout dress in the same colour. Hard hats are generally the rule, since this sport does entail fairly frequent accidents and it is very necessary to have head protection. Harness for this phase is usually much tougher than the harness used for dressage.

Cones This, in some respects, is a mixture of both the previous phases. The Whip is usually dressed in the clothes worn for the dressage phase and the harness and vehicle are also the same as used for dressage. However, the driving style used for the cones is more akin to that of the marathon section.

The important thing to remember is that the amount of physical, monetary and time commitment required for this discipline is enormous. Knowledge of equine husbandry is also essential, as is the discipline of keeping up with the ever-changing rules of the sport.

Scurry Driving

This, like combined driving, is a great sport and challenge. Sadly, too many people tend to put their animals into scurry driving before they have spent a few seasons schooling them in other disciplines. Progression should be rather like learning a musical instrument – the 'scales' come first (long-reining and basic schooling), 'classical pieces' follow (showing, rallies, everyday types of driving), then comes 'jazz' (FEI and scurry).

In an ideal world, before undertaking FEI and scurry, two or three seasons should be spent on a mixture of work similar to that of showing and rallies, to instil deep-seated discipline into the driving animals. In the long term, this pays off.

The style of driving used in scurry is an art in itself. Again, the Whip leans forward in the pelvis (known as sitting on the 'loo seat'), a rein in each hand – the whip as well as a rein in the right hand. Usually gloves and apron are worn in addition to a hat. The reins are buckled, so, to shorten them quickly (which needs doing *very* often) the hands 'do the splits' on them. In other words, the hands go out sideways which, in effect, slides the left hand forward up the nearside rein while the right hand goes forward up the offside rein. This effectively shortens the reins and yet they can be lengthened very quickly back to normal.

Practise makes perfect and short practises at home are not only great fun, but a good discipline for the quick reactions necessary for this aspect of the sport of driving. The animals have to be able to stop 'on a sixpence', go into gallop at a word command and be supple enough to turn sharp corners at speed without going down.

Driving for Disabled People

It is beyond doubt that there is a role for animals to play in the rehabilitation of the infirm, and equines are no exception. There are examples of carriages built in the nineteenth century that could take a wheelchair. King George IV, who had been a very bold Whip in his youth, had a low, wide-entrance Phaeton designed for him so that he could continue to drive, even though he was debilitated by gout. Hand-propelled bathchairs, widely used by the infirm who were 'taking the water' in the spa towns, were often fitted with shafts so that small ponies or donkeys could pull them. When she was elderly, Queen Victoria used a small pony Phaeton in the grounds of Osborne House, and drove a favourite white donkey herself.

More recently, HRH Prince Philip, who had given up polo and was enjoying driving, suggested to Sanders Watney, who was President of the British Driving Society, that disabled people could be taught to drive. This idea was put in turn to the Donkey Breed Society, and Mrs Nancy Pethick started to teach a group of people at Sandhurst, using donkeys and low, narrow floats. The BDS members immediately lent their help and expertise and, in 1973, staged a national sponsored drive which raised money for new carriages, which were very stable two-wheelers with low and easy entrance for the semi-ambulant. Each had a back which lowered to form a ramp, allowing a wheelchair and occupant to mount and travel securely within the carriage. These carriages were wide enough for an able-bodied helper to sit beside the disabled person, thus dispensing with the helper walking on the end of the headcollar rope. This meant that disabled people were free to drive at all paces wherever they chose!

In 1976 the fast-expanding Riding For The Disabled Association (RDA) extended its aims to include driving. It now gives the opportunity of riding and driving to any disabled person whose general health and happiness might benefit from these activities.

Driving as a sport as well as a therapy is now a highlight for many disabled people despite all kinds of disabilities of varying severity, including paraplegia. Disabled Whips have tested and proved themselves against able-bodied competitors admirably in the show ring, the dressage arena and across country. The sport of driving will open up to many more as the design of vehicles and their springing progresses.

Since driving can be dangerous, sensible safety precautions are taken by the RDA when arranging their group and individual sessions. An able-bodied companion is seated in the carriage beside the disabled Whip at all times and holds a separate pair of reins, enabling them to assist instantly if necessary, but they do not otherwise interfere with the Whip's control. It is important that the animal is carefully trained and is of a sensible and understanding disposition; a forward-going character who obeys instantly and willingly. Methods of holding the reins are as varied as the disabilities of those who hold them. The lack of hands or arms which behave in the usual way does not stop these carriage driving enthusiasts. Neither does lack of sight, hearing or speech prevent participation in this sport.

As can be seen from this list of activities, there are many different aspects to driving. However, they all have the same basic requirements: good, safe, obedient, well trained animals (be they horses, ponies or donkeys); safe, sound harness and vehicles which are correctly balanced and, most importantly, Whips who drive with knowledge and skill and are thoughtful and considerate toward other people and animals, especially when out on the roads.

A vehicle for disabled drivers.

CHAPTER 2

Choosing the Driving Animal

The acquisition of your first driving animal can have some very important connotations. When you have bought vehicles and harness to fit, you will almost certainly buy either the essential replacement animal or additional ones of the same size. Furthermore, you will discover that your first animal is best at a certain type of driving, whether showing, rallies, FEI competition or perhaps pottering with the family and, unless you have very clear ambitions, your driving will probably develop along the lines which suit your animal.

The first purchase of ours, almost by chance, was a 15 hh black cob with white socks and blaze. She was very sensible and adaptable but not very showy. She proved ideal for combining rally driving with light farm work and helped develop our conviction of the economic viability of such a horse in modern agriculture. Her kind nature encouraged us to start a driving school – still thriving with her successors – and her complete safety under all conditions led to the setting up of a wedding carriage service.

Our present horses, still the same size, colour and temperament, are now busy with weddings most Saturdays and are the third and fourth bought to match the original mare. The steadiness and adaptability of these horses has allowed them to be driven pair, tandem, trandem (three abreast), unicorn (two behind one) and team. So the selection of your first animal may have a profound effect upon your driving career.

Size

Perhaps the first decision should be the size of animal to buy, and your own temperament is the best guide there. Generally speaking, ponies have quicker movements and reactions than horses and we have discovered, having taught a wide range of people to drive with animals from 10 hh to 15.2 hh, that most people find that they are happiest with one particular size. The best way to discover the size which suits you is to try driving as many animals as possible before deciding to buy. You may find the quick reactions of a pony either stimulating or disconcerting and the long, steady stride of a horse either satisfying or dull.

The selection of the animal along these lines may, however, be something of a council of perfection; in many cases the size is forced upon you by other considerations. As mentioned earlier, many people start driving when their child's much loved riding pony is outgrown. If the thought of sale is unbearable, the alternative of driving may

The Shetland, though small, is strong. (If the Gig had a 'well bottom' or dropped floor, the Whip and groom would have a better sitting position and would not look so cramped.)

well be the answer. A pony of 11–12 hh although suitable for only a child to ride, is a very efficient size for two adults to drive. Pulling a vehicle is much less tiring for a pony than carrying a rider. If you doubt this, try carrying a bale of hay and then pushing it in a wheelbarrow! If the pony is to do double duty as both a child's riding pony and for driving,

then the riding requirement will decide the size in the same way as when a ride and drive animal is required for an adult.

Purchase For Specific Uses

The second consideration is the use for which the animal is required. For competition, the choice is simple; the size should be as close as possible to the upper limit for the class. The only exception to this is scurry driving, where the classes are under 12 hh and 12 hh and over. It is generally accepted that the ideal size in each class is as close as possible to 12 hh. In the show ring, it is sometimes thought that horses have an advantage over ponies, but we are not convinced that this is true and, in any case, there are usually separate classes, so they would only compete against each other in the championship. For rally driving, where a speed of 11 kph (7 mph) is required for about 12 miles, any size is suitable, although those under 12 hh will have to be fitter to compensate for their lack of size. If you wish to carry more than two people, especially in a four-wheeled vehicle, an animal of 14.2 hh or more is advisable.

If ambitions lie in the direction of driving pairs and teams, the ponies have the advantage of lower purchase price and are easier to transport. They are easier to match and should you decide on grey Welsh ponies of 12 –

13 hh, you will have much less of a problem in matching a team than most people!

Cost

This, inevitably, is a very important consideration. Ponies are significantly cheaper to drive than horses. Not only are they cheaper to buy, but they can be transported in comparatively small trailers behind cars instead of the Landrover-type vehicles or lorries needed for horses. Their harness (though not necessarily their vehicles) will also be cheaper. They will also need a little less food and grazing than horses.

Driving Donkeys

To get satisfaction from driving donkeys you need to be a rather special person. You must not take yourself too seriously and must be prepared to be made a fool of. This is not because donkeys are stubborn and stupid as some people still think, but because of the basic difference between donkeys and horses or ponies. In the wild, because donkeys are not so fast as horses or ponies, they cannot rely on their speed for safety on the plains. Instead, they rely on their agility on mountains where the grazing is too sparse to support a herd, and each donkey must be responsible for his own safety rather than following the lead of the chief stallion. Donkeys are also equipped with loud voices and big ears to communicate over long distances, and feet where the sole grows with the hoof wall to provide better wear on the rocks.

These natural characteristics govern the successful approach to driving a donkey. Their need to provide for their own safety means that you cannot gain their obedience by taking the place of the 'lead stallion'. Instead, you must encourage them to convince themselves of the safety of a situation. Where you would rely on the obedience of a horse, you must gain the co-operation of a donkey. This improves your understanding of psychology and your patience and you will probably agree that donkeys are more intelligent than horses and ponies. If you are able to reach this happy state, you will find great pleasure in driving donkeys.

Experience has proved it possible to train and drive a quadriga of donkeys; a highly memorable episode. Perhaps the greatest pleasure is driving them down the road unshod – since their hard-wearing feet will take about 11 km (7 miles) a week on roads without shoes – in almost total silence. It is rather like jogging, without the effort!

Temperament

A kind, steady temperament combined with boldness and courage is essential for a harness animal. Most of these characteristics are genetically inherited, but they are accentuated to their advantage or disadvantage by the way in which the animal is trained and handled from birth.

The breeds available in the British Isles which are generally considered to be unsuitable for harness work are the Thoroughbred and pure-bred Arab. There are always exceptions and Thoroughbreds and Arabs *have* proved excellent for driving, but their numbers are very much in the minority, compared to the Welsh and other native breeds.

Welsh x Arab and Welsh x Thoroughbred crosses produce attractive driving animals, though the temperament can still be rather explosive. Welsh x Hackney is also popular and is, in many ways, one of the most attractive types of animal for private driving.

The native ponies such as Shetland, Highland, Exmoor, Connemara, Dales, Fell, Dartmoor and their crosses are usually excellent animals for everyday family driving, provided that they have been sensibly schooled. A good temperament is complemented by good sound schooling and safe, considerate handling thereafter. The good harness animal will stand immobile when instructed by the handler, even in times of dire emergency, but he does need the necessary in-built calm temperament, backed up by sound training.

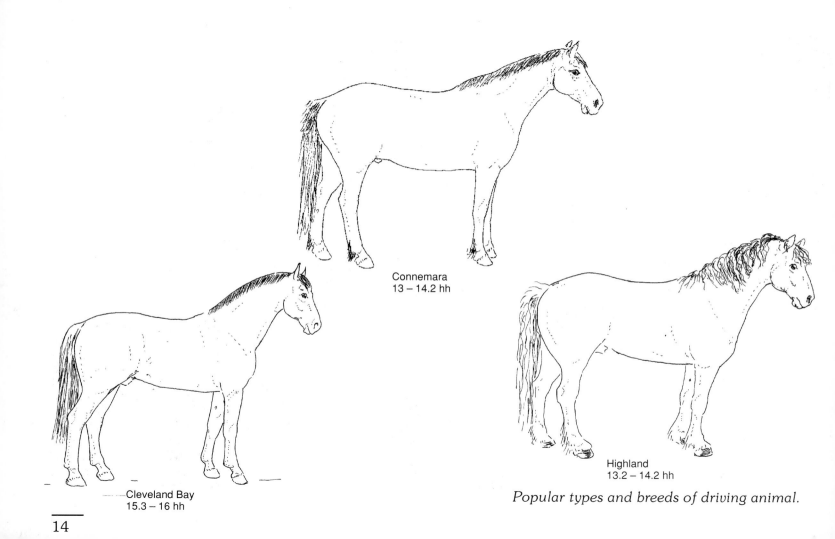

Connemara
13 – 14.2 hh

Cleveland Bay
15.3 – 16 hh

Highland
13.2 – 14.2 hh

Popular types and breeds of driving animal.

Welsh mountain pony not
exceeding 12 hh

Hackney, classes for:
ponies under 12.2 hh
ponies 12.2 – 14 hh
horses 14 – 15 hh
horses over 15 hh

Fell
13.2 hh

Shetland
40 – 42 inches

Dartmoor
Up to 12.2 hh

Welsh pony not
exceeding 13.2 hh

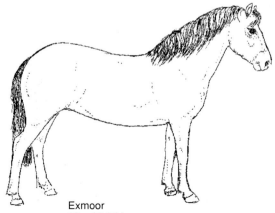

Exmoor
12 – 12.2 hh

Welsh pony of cob type not
exceeding 13.2 hh

Dales
Up to 14.2 hh

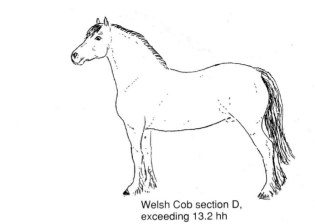

Welsh Cob section D,
exceeding 13.2 hh

New Forest
12 – 14.2 hh

Gelderlander
15.2 – 16.2 hh

17

Conformation and Movement

Conformation is also a matter that must be given serious consideration.

Usually an animal with good conformation can work more efficiently and attractively than one with poor conformation.

When purchasing a driving animal, it is important to check the following points:
1) Head, set on of neck and shoulders.
2) Shape of quarters, and setting on of tail.
3) Heart room and depth of ribcage.
4) Set on of legs, short cannons, good knees and hocks.
5) Good feet.
6) Movement.

The old saying that a good driving animal 'should have the head of a duchess and the backside of a pastry cook' is very true, inasmuch as a well set on neat head (with a good 'bold' eye) can be carried easily at the correct angle, whereas a large, heavy, common head cannot. The round, bold eye usually denotes a kind temperament; a small 'pig' eye is more likely to indicate a mean temperament. The neck should be of good length and well set on to a good sloping shoulder. The quarters (backside) need to be strong, not goose-rumped; good strong stifles and hocks are also essential.

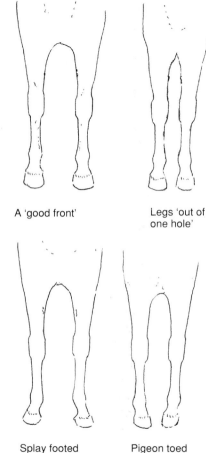

A 'good front'   Legs 'out of one hole'

Splay footed   Pigeon toed

Good and bad conformation of the forelegs.

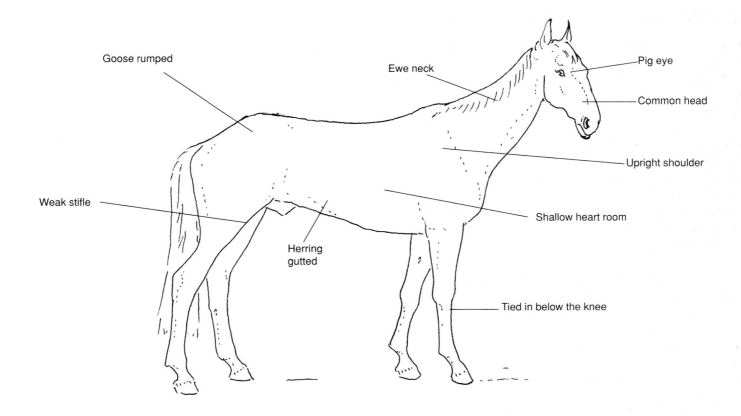

Goose rumped

Ewe neck

Pig eye

Common head

Upright shoulder

Weak stifle

Shallow heart room

Herring
gutted

Tied in below the knee

Features of poor conformation.

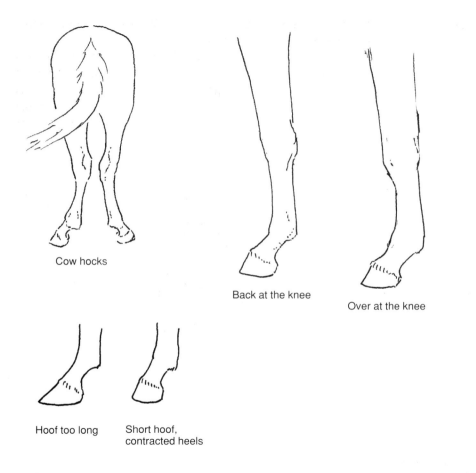

Cow hocks

Back at the knee

Over at the knee

Pasterns too long
and too sloping

Pasterns too short
and too upright

Hoof too long

Short hoof,
contracted heels

Good hoof/pastern axis –
45 degrees of slope

Conformation of the lower limbs.

The legs need to be four-square, that is one at each corner, and there must be plenty of heart room.

Ideally, all horses, ponies and donkeys should 'track straight', not forging, dishing or plaiting. Some of these problems may be caused by faulty foot care from the time of foaling, or by breaking in when too young, or too hurriedly. This means that the animal is schooled too hard and in too short a time for the tendons and muscles to become hard and fit. Sadly, this has, in recent years, become a very common fault in the schooling of harness animals. In the 'old days', schooling for saddle and harness was done over a minimum of six months, but nowadays some people seem to think that a week or even less (especially if the animal is kind-natured) is sufficient and so we see legs which 'blow up' or produce spavins and other disorders.

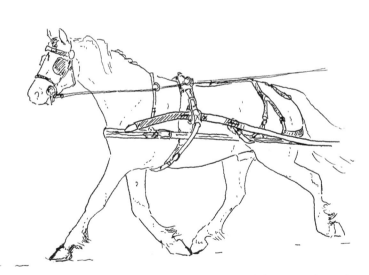

Forging occurs when the toe of the hind foot strikes the toe of the forefoot because the animal is unbalanced.

Dishing: the foreleg moves outward as it moves forwards.

However, if the training is done sensibly over a period of time, with plenty of slow, steady work, especially using hills, the quarter muscles of the animal develop properly. It is important to remember that the power of the draught animal comes from the quarters. It is the hind legs and quarter muscles which, in fact, provide the pulling power, as well as the braking power for going down hills and stopping.

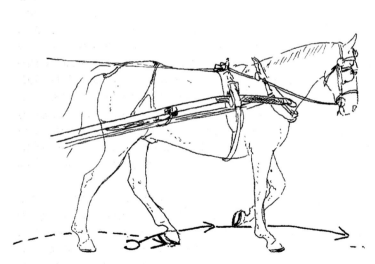

Overtracking; the hind foot steps in front of the print left by the corresponding forefoot.

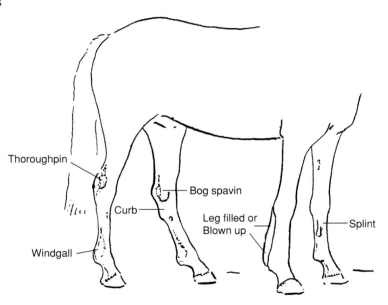

Thoroughpin

Bog spavin

Curb

Windgall

Leg filled or Blown up

Splint

Leg disorders caused by schooling a horse too hard and in too short a time.

CHAPTER 3

Care of the Driving Animal

To produce a fit harness animal takes time, patience and common sense as well as knowledge of feeding.

Achieving Fitness

For some very peculiar reason, far too many people expect their ponies to spend several weeks at a time at grass in the summer, yet to be ready to drive 26 km (16 miles) at a fast trot on a Sunday when they are taken to a rally. The owners then blame the poor animal if he becomes unsound in wind or limb or develops harness rubs. We do not expect a human to run in a marathon once or twice a month without a carefully planned exercise regime and a sensible diet, and we all know what would happen if he did. Why should a horse, pony or donkey be different? True, driving does not place as much strain on the joints, tendons and muscles of an animal as riding but, even so, a planned, sensible routine should be undertaken to get fit an animal who has come up from grass.

The traditional method of bringing up a hunter is still really the best and safest way. Regular worming is important to begin with and, if the animal is over eight years old, it is sensible to have the vet make an annual check on teeth. To start with, it can also be sensible to bring in during the day and turn out at night.

To get a horse or pony fit after a three month lay-off on grass, one should ideally allow eight weeks, starting with long-reining and lungeing on the first day, to remind him of commands and general manners. The farrier, who should have been called at least twice during the rest period to check and trim the hooves, is needed to fit new shoes to start work.

From the second day onwards, twenty minutes long-reining, with plenty of walking should, if possible, be followed by riding at walk only for half an hour. (Riding is preferable for early fitness work, although this can be done from a trap.) By the end of the first week, exercise time can be increased to an hour, but still only walking.

For the second and third weeks, the animal should still be only walking but the time can be increased gradually up to an hour and a half. After three or four weeks, increase the time to two hours (still walking) but if at all possible, include some work up and down hills to develop the muscles, especially those of the hindquarters.

In the fifth and sixth weeks, start some trotting sessions; trot 0.8 km (½ mile), walk 1.6 km (1 mile) and repeat and then trot a little further and gradually build up the trotting distance until you are able to trot 6–8 km (4–5 miles) steadily. By the end of the seventh or eighth week, your animal should have good hard legs, good wind and strong heart muscles and be fit for all everyday driving activities. An animal who is to be used for FEI competition or long distance driving will, of course, require a longer fitness programme to build up the extra stamina demanded by these sports.

Basic Signs of Fitness and Unfitness

Fitness:

Alert eyes, pricked ears, head carried alertly.

Coat smooth and bright.

In a fit animal, the ribs should be just visible, but the rest of the animal should have good hard muscles with well fleshed quarters, good neck and shoulder muscles.

The droppings should be formed, not sloppy and not bullet hard.

The neck should have a slight hard crested curve to it.

Unfitness:

Dull eyes and drooping ears, hanging head.

Harsh, rough coat.

Ribs showing, poor fleshing on quarters.

Soft muscles.

Scouring or constipation.

Dirty nose.

The Coat

Whilst carrying out the fittening programme, it is very important to get the animal's coat really clean and supple by regular, thorough grooming. Extra emphasis should be placed upon those areas which will be subject to pressure from the harness: the girth, collar, breeching etc. It is obviously essential to continue giving attention to these areas when the animal is being driven regularly, and to keep the harness clean and supple, in order that sores and galling are avoided.

Principles of Feeding

While this fitness programme is being carried out, it is essential that safe and sensible feeding is practiced in line with the work being done.

If we say that the animal is to be in during the day and out at night for the driving season, this would probably reflect how the average family driving animal is kept during the summer. Remember, it will cause great discomfort to an animal to drive on a full stomach, especially if full of hard food, so when he comes in from the field, give just a small token feed in his stable and a very limited amount of hay. Allow at least an hour and preferably rather longer before work starts. This is why, in the old days, the carters' horsemen used to start stables with feeding at 5 a.m. to allow time for digestion before work started at 7 a.m.

In racing and hunting yards, the first hard feed of the day is still very early and, when the horses are really fit and working hard, the total ration of hard food is split into a daily total of three feeds – sometimes four or five, starting at 6 a.m. with the last feed being at 8 or 9 p.m. Although this is not usually done for the average family driving pony, it could still be very necessary in the top FEI team yards, where the extra stamina needed comes from a steady programme of exercise and feeding.

Bear in mind that food is not fed to get the animal fit; the exercise does that. It is therefore important not to increase feed in advance of increasing work. Food fed after work done refuels ready for work the next day. So, for example, after the first small feed of the morning, the next feed would be given after returning from exercise, provided that the animal is cool and relaxed. If it is just walking exercise, then 0.5–1 kg (1–2 lb) of a balanced mix lightly damped would be fed, followed by a light feed of hay. If the work is trotting and the animal is now three-quarters fit, a further feed an hour or so before turning out might well be required.

Regarding choice and quantity of feed, a great deal does depend on the type and condition of grazing available and the type of animal. Native ponies will invariably do all that is required of them off grass alone, while a Thoroughbred cross will need some help from hard feed. It is, nonetheless, safer to underfeed hard food rather than overfeed. Too much hard food may cause toxaemia and encourage over-excitment, which can cause accidents.

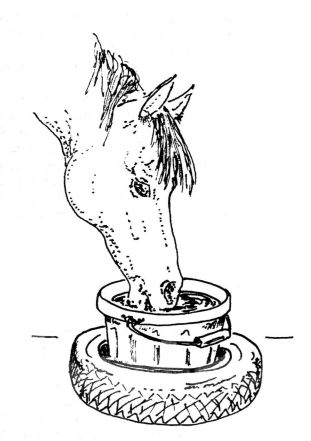

Basic foodstuffs include broad bran, molassed chaff, rolled oats, sugar beet, haylage, rolled barley, and coarse mix or nuts, of which there are many brands. Some have a low protein content, while others are rather high in protein. Mixing one's own feed is not always convenient, so most people nowadays tend to use the complete mixes or nuts. The former take longer for the animals to eat, which usually means they chew the food more thoroughly, and this will help alleviate the boredom which can lead to stable vices.

Good, clean hay is essential. Equines have a rather peculiar digestive system. The actual stomach is quite small – for a 15 hh horse it is only the size of a football – and, since this is where the hard food is digested, small individual feeds are appropriate. Hay and roughage, however, are digested in the main gut and it is when the animal goes for long periods of time without roughage, or has irregular feeding times, that horrors like twisted guts and severe colic occur, so it is important to establish a regular feeding routine when the animal is stabled.

A supply of clean water should be permanently available.

To prevent spillage, a bucket of water or feed can be stood in an old tyre or two.

CHAPTER 4

Training the Animal to go in Harness

Training, schooling, breaking to harness – whatever name is put to this exercise, it is probably the next most important factor to the actual choice of animal.

No matter how superb the conformation or temperament of the animal, it can all be totally wasted or ruined by bad or indifferent schooling. The saying that 'you get back what you put in' is very true in this instance. Yes, some animals do take longer to train than others, and this applies to humans as well! Sadly, many well trained animals go on to homes where they become spoilt by the way they are handled and worked. This is often the result of pure inexperience on the part of the owner. The mixture of a novice owner and a novice animal is a recipe for problems, and can be disastrous.

Professional Schooling

Very often these days, the first animal used by a family for driving is the outgrown children's pony, whose reschooling to harness will be a new venture for all concerned.

Many owners wisely choose to send their beloved animal to a professional harness trainer, of whom there are a good number. However, it is important to stress that careful checking of the reputation of the chosen establishment should be carried out well beforehand and, if possible, a visit should be made to ensure that the animals in residence look calm and contented. If it is possible to watch some basic training, such as long-reining, you can assess to some degree what kind of relationship the trainer is establishing with their animals or pupils.

It is also a good idea to go to some shows and/or rallies where there is driving, and to consider the type of temperament and presence you would like your animal to end up with. Then, when the decision is made as to where the pupil is going for training, you can ask that he is trained to move off slowly (which is always preferable). Many yards do train for a brisk move-off and, once learnt, it can be difficult to break this habit.

Before he comes home from the yard where he is being trained to drive, it is advisable to have at least one hour with your animal and the person who is doing the training. This will enable you to hear the words of command your animal has learnt and it will be helpful for the future to watch his degree of obedience and co-operation.

When you have got your animal home, it is always a wise and safe precaution to spend quite a while each day long-reining before you put to. This will enable you both to understand each other and you will find it easier to use your own way of giving commands to your animal, who has to adapt what he has heard before to your way of saying the same thing. This can be especially true of the words 'Trot on'. Many ladies seem to put an 'e' after the first 't', so that the sound is 'Terot'; quite different from a brisk 'Trot on'.

Training at Home

A great many animals are trained at home, and very well too. However, there are some who, because of their kind, peaceful temperaments, encourage their owners to cut too many corners in basic schooling. Let us look at how a training programme *should* proceed.

The Blinkered Bridle and Driving Bit

Getting a riding animal used to the restrictions of blinkers is probably one of the more difficult tasks, inasmuch as calmness and patience must prevail. Introducing the animal to the driving bridle is best done in the stable with the halter fastened round the neck and the animal tied up. It is important at this stage that the cheekpieces are not too short, so that there isn't a battle to get the headpiece over the ears.

A Liverpool bit, or a reversible (elbow) bit will normally be used. These two bits are considered to be the most suitable for driving, because of the presence of the curb chain, if needed, to avoid an accident. The chosen bit can be wrapped with sticking plaster with some honey on it to help acceptance by an animal who has previously been ridden in a snaffle. The importance of the correct adjustment of bit and curb chain will be dealt with in Chapter 9.

When the animal is learning to accept the bridle, it is a good idea to leave him tied up by a headcollar with the bridle on for ten minutes the first day, more on the second day and so on, for a few days more.

Long-reining

At the same time as having lessons on the wearing of the blinkered bridle, long-reining with an open bridle can begin, to teach the animal obedience to word command and steering from the ground.

If the animal was broken-in for riding in the correct, traditional manner, he will have already learnt the basic facts of long-reining. Sadly, not all training is done thoroughly nowadays and many animals have never had more than a little lungeing, if that. Long-reins fitted in the draw rein position for schooling can help to teach collection and good movement from the beginning. Bearing reins may also be used by experienced trainers to help get the head at the right angle, but do remember to do this only for a short time to begin with; it can cause distress if overdone.

One can usually find out quite quickly whether the correct training has been done in the past. If not, ask someone (not a small child), to lead the animal on a lead rope while you, the trainer, walk behind with the long-reins.

Once obedience to the voice commands 'Whoa', 'Stand' and 'Walk on' is achieved, proceed to teach obedience to 'Trot on'. Just before this point of the long-rein schooling it is a good idea to make sure you can lunge on long-reins and get the obedience you are looking for. For the initial schooling in long-reins, pass the reins through the stirrups on a saddle or through the loops of a driving pad. For the later stages of schooling, pass the reins through the terrets. Do remember to use a firm, positive voice at all times.

When the animal is obedient to commands, take him out on the road in long-reins to meet traffic. Again, take assistance in case it is needed for dealing with lorries, tractors etc.

The more work done from the ground with long-reins the better, and even when your animal is really fit and used to driving, two or three sessions of long-reining each week is advisable. Also, once the animal is fit, he can be kept fit with between twenty and thirty minutes a day lungeing on long-reins. It is not necessary to ride or drive every day to maintain fitness, and, in fact, long-reining can help prevent boredom and staleness. It also enables you to see how the animal looks in terms of outline and movement.

Overbent and behind the bit. The animal is looking at the ground, not where he is going.

Above the bit. Energy going up with the back hollowed; the animal cannot pull without straining his back.

On the bit. Horse looking where he is going, energy going forward. The forward movement can be controlled into collection (left) or extension (right).

Further training for the horse and the eye of the Whip.

Collar and Traces

Once you are satisfied that your animal is obedient to voice commands, then the time has come to fit collar and traces. To start with, it is preferable to do this in a yard or corner of a paddock.

The collar is put on (obviously, if a full collar is used, it has to be put on before the bridle, see Chapters 8 and 9). For driving, the breast collar should also go on before the bridle but, when training, it may be necessary for the animal to stand tied up with the training bridle on for twenty minutes or so before the first lesson in draught takes place.

Also, twenty minutes long-reining beforehand is a sensible idea. Do remember that the breast collar should lie at least 2.5 cm (1 in) above the point of shoulder (see illustration page 67).

Extend the traces with baling string or lightweight rope, webbing or some similar material and, with the help of two assistants, one on each trace, ask the animal to walk on. As he moves forward, ask the helpers to start pulling gently on their individual traces so that he starts to go 'into his collar'.

While this is being done, talk calmly to the animal to give him confidence and do remember to praise him. Ponies, horses and donkeys are not machines; they have feelings and are usually thinking animals. Far too may people forget this.

However, to be too soft with them is a great fault, so kind but firm handling is important in order to achieve basic obedience. The two things go together – the aim is real teamwork.

Pulling a Tyre, Log or Harrow

The next stage is to put an inanimate object, rather than two human beings, behind the traces. A tyre is one of the easiest objects to obtain and it is fairly quiet when pulled. However, the scratching noise of a tyre on tarmac, concrete or gravel is a good start for the animal to get used to noises coming from behind.

It can be a good, even if rather hilarious, exercise to have your animal tied up and let him watch you pull the tyre around. Once he looks totally bored, then it is his turn! If a tyre is not available, then a suitably sized log or harrow can be used.

When you are happy that all is going well (and this should be over quite a number of lessons, not just one or two), then the day comes to let the animal view a vehicle, preferably a strong and safe exercise/breaking-in vehicle. Introduce this – as far as possible – as you did with the tyre.

Putting To for the First Time

See Chapter 8 and 9 for details of correct fittings of harness and putting to for a single.

For this procedure, it is important to have at least one competent helper on whom you can really rely. Once you have put to and everything is fitted correctly, but while your animal is still tied up, gently move the vehicle backwards and forwards so that the animal feels the breeching come into play. In addition to the pull on the collar, make some banging noises with a can or something similar behind so that the noise sounds like the thumps and squeaks one can often hear when driving. Once he is calm about all this, you can proceed to the exciting bit, which will show whether you have done your training correctly and your animal trusts you.

Moving Off

Do this, in the first instance, by long-reining from the ground, with a helper at the animal's head. This is a safety precaution. It is also useful at this point for the helper to have the animal on a lunge line, fitted so that it goes through the nearside ring of the bit, over the headpiece, and is attached to the offside ring of the bit. If, horror of horrors, the animal decides it is far too dangerous an adventure after all, this arrangement will enable the helper to pull him into a circle as if lungeing to prevent him from bolting. The main thing is that the person on the ground long-reining from the side or back of the trap should be in charge of steering.

In order that the whole thing does not turn over, it is a useful idea for this first stage of driving to be done in a reasonably confined space, such as a yard, or a drive at the end of which there is a good solid building. This will prevent any full-blown bolting.

Driving from the Vehicle

Once you are satisfied that everything is going correctly and the animal seems happy, then the moment for driving from the coachman's seat arrives. However, still keep your helper at the head with the lunge line fitted for emergency collection. Proceed to mount (see Chapter 10), take up your reins and ask the animal to walk on.

Once you are reasonably sure that you are in control, that the animal is calm and listening to you with his ears tilted back, then it is time for your helper to unhitch the lunge rein and join you in the vehicle.

Do always remember to watch the ears and the head-carriage of your pony, horse or donkey when driving. You have no animal underneath you to enable you to feel the slightest twinge of apprehension, so it is only your observation and anticipation which can help you to avoid problems. When the animal lifts his head or pricks his ears well forward, he is telling you that there is something around that he is not happy about. Similarly it is up to you, when you spot something that may cause concern to your animal, to tell him in a calm but firm voice to walk or trot on, and to keep doing so until the problem is passed. This way, you are attracting the attention of the well schooled, obedient animal, telling him to do as he is told, rather than worry about dangers, or even imaginary problems like dustbins and manhole covers.

For the first few months of driving a freshly schooled animal it is sensible to wear a 'Safety – Caution' vest. This will usually encourage drivers of other vehicles to be more considerate, but do remember always to thank motorists for their care, even those who are inconsiderate. Often they do not understand the dangers of frightening animals, and sometimes they can learn good manners from the horse world!

From this starting point, it is up to you to practise steady, safe driving with your newly schooled animal. Do not go rushing off showing, or to FEI events, until you have found out how your animal behaves when out with other turnouts. As with hunters and gymkhana ponies, a driving animal will 'hot up' in company until he is used to it. Although it can be hard to exercise patience at this stage because you want to show everyone how clever you and your animal are, remember that practise makes perfect and patience is a virtue.

CHAPTER 5

Dress and Equipment

The details of traditional wear for the show ring are discussed in Chapter 14; The Show Ring. The following is, for the moment, a basic guide to factors affecting safety and comfort.

Dress

While choice of clothes for general driving is entirely up to the individual, some guidelines will perhaps be helpful. One may take the attitude that any old thing will do for exercise and around the stable yard, but even here there must be some regard for the safety angle. Sandals, particularly of the flip-flop variety, comfortable though they may be, offer no protection from iron-shod feet, and the lack of heel may cause a disaster on a carriage step, as might a high or shaped heel. A loosely knitted jumper or legwarmers invite curb hooks and buckles to get entangled in them, as does any garment featuring the slashed or torn look. Whether it is for hot or cold weather, practicability and tidiness need to be the watchwords for clothing. Where there is pride in the turnout of horse and carriage this will extend to the Whip, groom and passengers.

Knee Rugs and Driving Aprons

The purpose of knee rugs is to keep the Whip and passengers warm and dry. They were traditionally made from the same box cloth as the cushions and the fall and lining of the folding head, and were an integral part of the carriage. These rugs were lined with a warm blanket material using a subdued check or a subtle colour. Waterproofed material or lightweight leather were also used to make both rugs and carriage aprons.

An individual knee rug needs to be large enough to be double at the back because sitting on the wrapover holds it in place. A coaching rug was wide enough to cover all four passengers on a seat and, to prevent it falling, a fixed loop or 'D' was used with a strap buckling it to the backrest.

On early travelling carriages and Phaetons, a soft leather apron was fitted snugly from the foot of the dash up over the lap and was held in place by loops and little button stops or studs shaped into the back and side rails of the seats for this purpose.

Driving Whips

A whip should always be carried in the hand whilst driving. It is an aid which is used to help and guide far more than to chastise. It is also possible to communicate with other drivers through signalling with it, indeed, in the 'old days' the coachmen had a whole whip 'language' with which to 'talk' to each other.

Types of Whip

Traditional styles of whip used in the past were drop-thong or dealer's, carter's or waggoner's and bow-top for coaching and carriage work, smart trade and private driving.

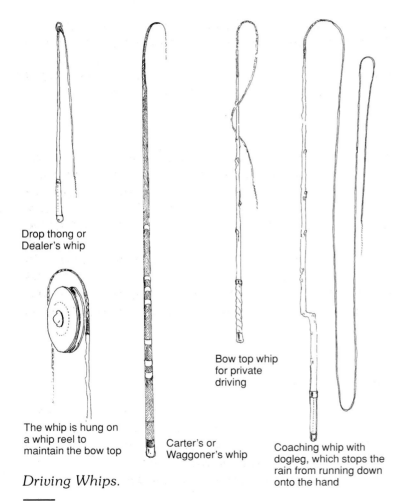

Drop thong or
Dealer's whip

The whip is hung on
a whip reel to
maintain the bow top

Driving Whips.

Bow top whip
for private
driving

Carter's or
Waggoner's whip

Coaching whip with
dogleg, which stops the
rain from running down
onto the hand

Drop-thong or dealer's whip. The strong, flexible stock was made from whalebone or a spring steel wire sandwiched and glued between split cane, all encased in a woven thread tube. This tapering, flexible stock finished in a loop from which the hide thong hung down. The thong was made from square-cut rawhide or six-plait horsehide finished in a whipcord lash.

Carter's or waggoner's whip. This was made in the same way as the dealer's whip but was much longer (up to 1.9 m – 6 ft) and more robust as it was used mostly from the ground. It tapered off to a wispy end. The butt end had a heavy brass mount, and many brass collars or ferrules about 2.5 cm (1 in) deep were used to strengthen and enhance it.

Coaching, carriage and Gig whips. All these were made to a similar style but varied in weight and length to allow for personal preference and for the type of carriage they were to be used with.

A lady driving a pony to a Gig would have used a light whip with a fairly short reach. This would perhaps have had an ornate handle made from ivory (or celluloid made to look like ivory) with an ornate collar and butt sometimes made from silver.

A coaching whip's stock has to be longer and stronger both for reach and support. The 3.7 m (12 ft) long six-plait horsehide thong was quite heavy, particularly when waterlogged and whisking through the air. The stocks were made from various woods; holly, blackthorn, yew, willow and bamboo were used. The handle was sometimes wrapped in a lead ribbon under the leather finish to help with the balance. The top end of the stick tapered off into a thin and supple end where the thong was spliced to it with goose quill supports bound with black waxed thread, so making the bow-shaped top. The thong was finished in an inconspicuous lash made from whipcord, cotton silk or raffia.

Choice of Whip

If kicking is not to be promoted, the whip must be used between the collar and pad. When it needs to be used it must be applied instantly and must therefore always be ready in the hand. To sit happily in the hand the diameter of the handle needs to be a comfortable fit and the whole whip nicely balanced. If it should be top-heavy, the stick will droop down tiring the wrist and hand; balance can be helped by weighting the butt end in some way.

The modern whip made from synthetic materials usually has a smooth surface with no gnarls or twig joints such as natural holly and thorn wood have. Because there is nothing to catch and hold the thong up along the stick, the long thong falls over the hand and this can be awkward – if not dangerous – while driving. One way to prevent this from happening is to have some strategically placed rings made

from a toning brown velcro glued to the stick, with a few tiny pieces stitched to the thong. This will allow the whip to be folded and carried in a traditional-looking way, but the lash will unfold with the force of the stick being brought backwards quickly, ready for the forward throw.

Care of the Whip

The working whip has to withstand many abuses – being caught in hedges and trees, run over, sat upon and thrown down in the strangest of places. The modern nylon or plastic-fibre whip can put up with all this, but the traditional type needs to be treated with respect and preserved for the show ring and special days. To keep the bowed top in its nice curve it must be hung up clear of the floor on a whip reel, with the end part of the stick and quill curved around the wheel, which has a groove in it to grip the bow top. The thong can be kept clean with a soapy sponge, and soft with mutton fat.

Spares

Even though we are unlikely to be as far from help as in the old coaching days, when the boot of a coach was equipped to deal with just about any eventuality, it is still essential to carry spares and know how to use them.

If the harness and carriage are properly matched and

well maintained, the likelihood of a breakage is reduced, but accidents do happen.

A strap is most likely to break at the hole where the buckles put a strain. If the rule of never working in the last hole is observed there will always be one left to get you home. With a few readjustments of other straps the animal should still be able to work comfortably.

A sharp knife, some string and a pocket handkerchief or neck scarf are items which will solve most problems. Hopefully, the knife will be used not to cut the harness but the string. The handkerchief can alleviate a rub or can make a pressure pad to stop bleeding.

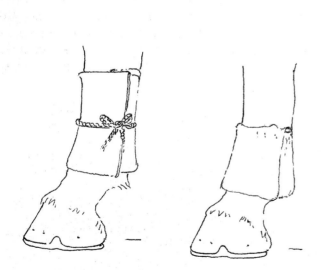

Temporary brushing boots made from a handkerchief fastened with string.

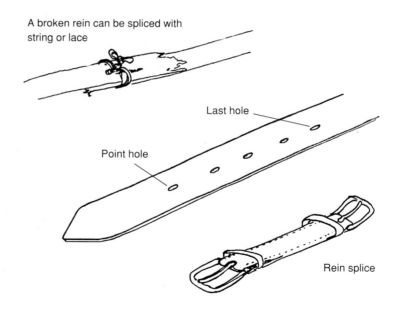

A broken rein can be spliced with string or lace

Last hole

Point hole

Rein splice

Running repairs on broken reins.

Considerable thought must go in to assembling the most appropriate spares kit, but the following is a list of basics:

Knife
String
Hoofpick
Matches (for candle lamps)
Trace that fits
Leather punch
Leather lace
Rein splice

String gloves
Wound powder
Fly repellent
Small change
    (for telephone, etc.)
Vet's telephone number
Personal identification
    and blood group

This collection should be kept tidily in an accessible place so that if something is needed it will be in full view. Having to rummage through a dark bag can make a simple problem into an emotional drama! Ingenious containers for displaying spares have been developed almost to an art form, and some cost a lot of money, but a clear, strong polythene bag will serve its purpose.

When driving in dull conditions a tabard, belt or anklets made from Dayglo reflective material should be worn either by the Whip, groom or animal, or fitted to the back of the carriage. This will help other road users to see the turnout in good time. A dark-coloured animal with a natural varnished or dark carriage, and people wearing country clothing blend into the background better than many military camouflages.

CHAPTER 6

The Groom

The groom is a very important person. It used to be said that 'a coachman was only as good as his man on the ground', and this is probably as true today as it ever was.

An employed groom is responsible for bringing the driving animals to the carriage fit and well, and in a frame of mind to work happily and obediently, and also for producing the carriage and harness safely and neatly maintained with the animals correctly put to. Nowadays, in the do-it-yourself era, these duties may be shared amongst family and friends. Even so, they are vitally important jobs and whoever does them should be valued and held in high esteem.

When holding the harnessed animal, the groom faces him holding the reins either side of the bit (never by the cross bar of a pair or team coaching bit). In this position the groom can see the animal(s) and protect him or them from any dangers coming from behind as, with the blinkers on, an equine cannot do so for himself. He can, however, see his trusted groom and is reassured by a quiet voice and presence close to his head. Also, in this position, close communication between Whip and groom is possible.

When the Whip is comfortably in place and has established contact, the groom is asked to release the reins (perhaps by a slight signal). He must now not touch them again unless the Whip invites this, just as a passenger in a car must never touch the steering wheel or controls. If, when on the ground, a groom takes hold of the reins, he first takes the contact from the Whip's hands before making contact with the bit. In that time, however brief, no-one is in charge. However, a groom on the ground can first speak soothingly or encouragingly to an animal and, when he is thus aware of the groom's presence, a hand can be placed on the neck or shoulder to help steady or guide. Fingers placed through the back of the noseband may be of help to both animal and Whip in a situation when the former needs steadying, while a groom running a little ahead may help give confidence. However, the groom should never attempt to pull a driving animal forward by the bridle, or he may be left with the bridle in hand and a loose animal!

When driving an inexperienced animal deliberately in a tricky situation such as a carnival, parade or cross-country, a headcollar can be left on under the bridle so that the groom can help safely if required.

It is always advisable to have an active groom in attendance even if in the guise of a companion. The skill of driving is in dealing with the situation before it ever arises, but a pleasant drive can become a drama in a trice and, if the groom has been chosen and dressed for decorative qualities only, the drama may turn into a disaster. The carriage groom should be also able to drive a little to help out in an emergency and the BDS test for grooms requires this skill to achieve a pass.

In the early nineteenth century a very capable but particularly small man called the 'Tiger' was the fashionable carriage groom used with a Cabriolet or sometimes a Curricle. Under his livery coat he wore a horizontally striped waistcoat denoting that he was a member of the outside staff. His smallness emphasised the size and magnificence of the Cabriolet Horse.

CHAPTER 7

Choice of Vehicle

It is doubtful whether the equal of the best vehicles from the past will ever be made again. This is not to suggest that the best of the present day carriage builders are lacking in skill. Indeed, if allowed to, they could produce work the equal of anything from the heyday of carriage building. Materials have improved greatly on those available in the past and the principles and control of operations such as spring tempering are much better understood now. However, labour rates in the past were so low in relation to the final value of the vehicle that far more time could be expended in the construction than would now be economic.

If a vehicle were to be built now to the original standards, the cost would be several times that of buying an original vehicle, and therefore uneconomic. Furthermore, even if this problem could be overcome, it is likely that lack of experience and practise would still prevent the reproduction of a Lawton, Windover or Offord.

These makers turned out many vehicles, probably no two of which were exactly alike and, over the years, they would find that one small modification produced a better vehicle and this modification would be incorporated in their future products. This process would be repeated time after time until a degree of perfection was reached that cannot now be equalled. Carriage builders of the time did not usually publicise the secrets which gave them an advantage over their competitors. Those who did write books on the subject, like John Phillipson and William Bridges Adams, unknowingly attributed their success to principles which can now be demonstrated to be false.

All this means that the art of producing vehicles of the very highest quality is lost and the remaining examples undervalued. They should prove to be a good investment and give the satisfaction of owning a genuine original vehicle. They are also usually more acceptable to the judge in showing classes, though the official ruling is that a modern vehicle of equal quality is just as acceptable. The disadvantages of these vehicles are their more costly maintenance and lesser strength when compared to modern vehicles.

Notwithstanding the above there are some very competent carriage builders about who, with the advantage of modern knowledge, are producing very good, safe vehicles. Those of traditional type have the problem of competing with their undervalued predecessors and therefore have to incorporate some economies. Those manufacturers who have embraced modern materials and design are producing vehicles which, for specialised uses like FEI competition, are greatly superior to those from the past. In the early days of this competition, original vehicles were used but fortunately this destruction has now ceased. The buyer should, however, be aware that there are several

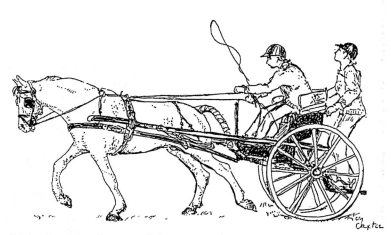

Vehicles are designed for special uses – a cross-country competition vehicle for single or tandem driving.

manufacturers currently operating who are lacking in ability, both as engineers and carriage builders. They are still producing vehicles which are unsafe and unsuitable for their purpose. The buyers' safeguard is to buy from a manufacturer of good reputation who is also, preferably, a carriage driver, and thus has some practical experience of the use of vehicles.

Features of a Good Vehicle

Let us look at some of the features present in a good vehicle.

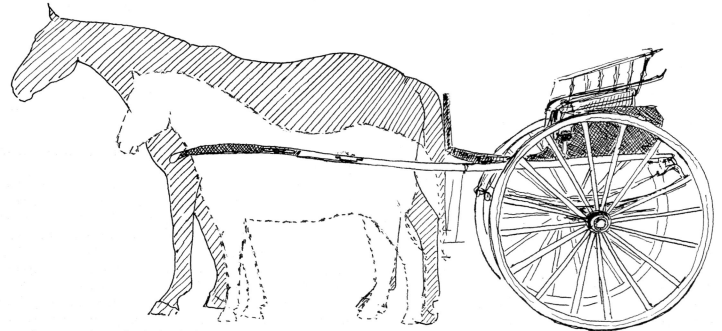

Not only must the vehicle be balanced – it must be neither over- nor under-horsed.

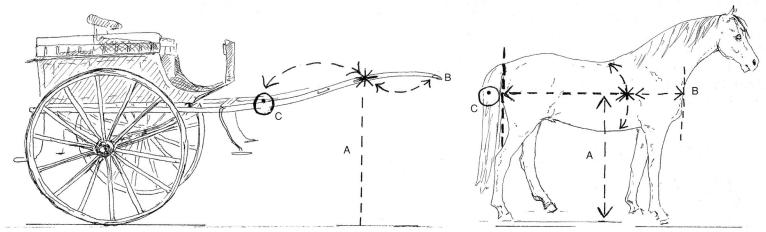

Corresponding measurements of driving animal and vehicle.

Balance

Taking a two-wheeler first, the most fundamental feature is balance. When the vehicle is loaded and the floor is level there should be a very light weight of about 1–2 kg (2–6 lb) on the shafts. The ideal weight depends upon the height of the trace attachment to the vehicle and the vehicle's rolling resistance. The object is to have just enough weight on the shafts to keep them resting in the tug loops when the animal is trotting if the shafts are sprung, or floating and making light contact with the bottom of the tug loops if unsprung. The higher the rolling resistance of the vehicle, the greater the tension in the traces and the greater this effect.

Any vehicle can be made to balance, either by moving the seat or the axle or, if all else fails, by loading weights in suitable places. The problem is, if heavy shafts are balanced by extra weight behind the axle, this extra weight, so far from the centre of gravity, produces moments of inertia which cause the vehicle to swing from side to side in use. Also, if the counterbalance weight consists of the passenger, the balance of the vehicle is going to be greatly changed when the passenger either mounts or dismounts.

The solution lies in a compromise of weight and strength in the shafts. The ideal is shafts which are flexible vertically and stiff laterally. These provide flexibility to even out the motion of the animal at the trot, and stiffness to resist the swing of the vehicle from side to side. This is especially noticeable downhill. The difficulty in the compromise lies in deciding how much strength is needed. If one could be certain that the vehicle would never be used unbalanced and that the Whip and passenger would always keep their weight towards the axle when mounting or dismounting, then the shafts could be kept so light as to work beautifully. However, some allowance must be made for abuse, and a compromise decided on. A cab-fronted

An example of balance – The heavy shafts of the Hansom Cab were balanced by seating the cabbie well back. The passengers, sitting over the axle, did not change the balance.

vehicle always has balance problems because of the weight of brackets and mountings required to attach the shafts. The best known of these vehicles, the Hansom Cab, overcame some of these problems cleverly by seating the driver who was, of course, always on board, well behind the axle to counterbalance the shafts. The passengers, who came and went, were seated over the axle and did not affect the balance.

The Shafts

The best material for shafts is lancewood which has, unfortunately, been unavailable for a long time, but may still be found in some old vehicles. It can be recognised by the shafts being unusually thin and the wood is so hard that it is impossible to screw into it without first drilling a hole. The best modern material is laminated ash and the worst – it has been used – is plywood! With this, of course, half the grain runs across the shafts. Many modern vehicles are fitted with steel tube shafts for economy. These can be reasonably satisfactory, although the inherent disadvantage is lack of flexibility. This can be improved by mounting the back of the shaft, and sometimes the front, onto a spring, as is often done with ash shafts to improve their flexibility and to reduce the shock loading on them. Fibreglass, because of its lightness and flexibility, should be very suitable for shafts, but appears to require further development to improve the ratio of vertical to horizontal flexibility.

However good the shafts are, they need to be correctly mounted to the vehicle. They should be allowed to flex throughout their length to provide the greatest flexibility and to reduce local loading. The practice of bolting the shafts to the underside of the seats on simple Governess Carts, especially if done with bolts through the shafts at the front of the vehicle, is little short of criminal. Ideally, the shafts should be hinged to the front of the vehicle and fastened here by clamps going right round the shafts, each located at the back by a spring. Here it is permissible to use a bolt through the shaft, since there is little loading on it at this point. This arrangement also provides positive fore and aft location of the shafts.

The shafts should remain wide apart where they run past the animal's quarters so as to provide room for the animal when turning. The highest and closest part of the shaft should be at the tug stops. This is the point of contact from which the animal controls the vehicle and the fit here is important. The shafts should extend forwards, outwards and downwards from the tug stops to a point level with the front of the animal's chest. This is important for safety and to allow the animal to turn easily without the reins catching over the shaft points. The exception to this is for FEI competition vehicles, where manoeuvrability can be improved by stopping the shafts just in front of the tug loops, provided that provision is made to prevent them from coming out of the tug loops.

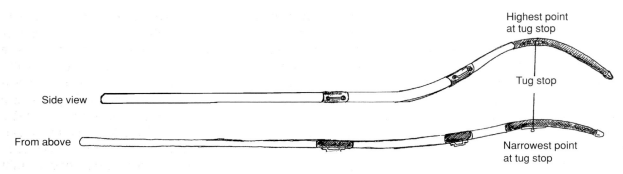

Side view

From above

Highest point
at tug stop

Tug stop

Narrowest point
at tug stop

Offside shaft viewed from side and above.

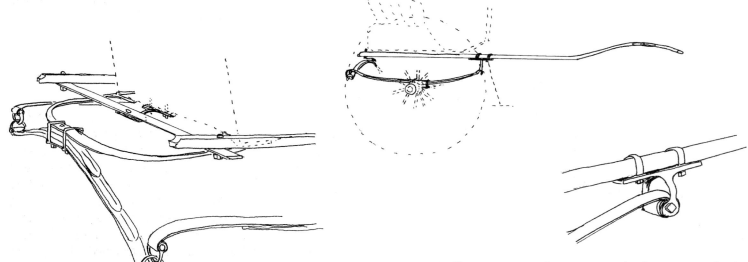

Different ways of springing shafts on to vehicles.

Wheels

Wheels are traditionally made with an angle between the spokes known as 'dish'. This gives the wheel the appearance of an umbrella opened almost flat and considerably increases the strength of a wooden wheel. When cornering, the weight of the vehicle is thrown largely onto the outside wheel (or wheels) and the tendency for the wheel to collapse under the vehicle is resisted by the tension of the iron wheel rim, which prevents the spokes going 'over-centre'. In order for the wheel to have maximum strength for carrying weight, the lower spoke must be vertical and this can only be achieved by sloping the end of the axle down at the same angle as the dish. This, in turn, causes the wheel to slide further onto the axle until stopped by the leather washer between the wheel and the collar on the axle. This needs to be kept well oiled to prevent excessive friction. An ingenious solution to this end loading is to use a tapered axle with the lower face horizontal. Unfortunately, the increased diameter of the axle causes as much friction as the end loading and such axles were usually used only on farm carts. Although modern steel wheels with taper roller bearings avoid these problems they are usually still built with dish. This is mainly for appearance, since they would be strong enough even if flat.

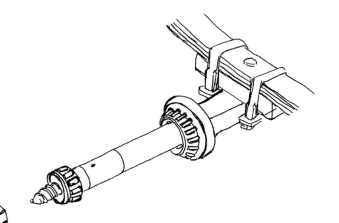

Modern axle with roller bearings.

The Body

The body of the vehicle may be of many different styles, but it should always give a good driving position with the feet at right angles to the shins and well forward, the thighs sloping downwards and the hands level with the animal's back. As a rule of thumb, the tops of the wheels should be level with the seat and the dashboard or rein rail level with the animal's back. If a breast collar is to be used, a swingle tree will be a great comfort to the animal. A less effective but still useful alternative is a splinter bar fitted with sprung trace hooks.

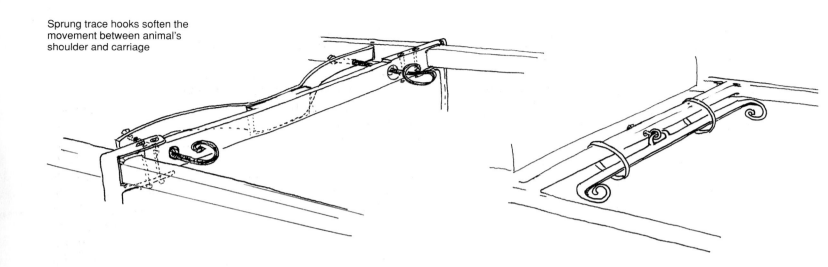

Sprung trace hooks soften the movement between animal's shoulder and carriage

When used with a breast collar and traces, a swingle tree evens out the movement of the animal's shoulder, making the drive smoother and more comfortable for animal, Whip and passenger.

The loose straps prevent the swingle tree from falling onto the hocks and frightening the animal – which might happen if the centre pivot breaks.

Special Features

Vehicles for FEI competition are becoming ever more specialised, with the aim of producing the most manoeuvrable, stable and easy-to-pull vehicle possible. Some ideas like rear steps on two-wheelers, which allow the groom full side–to–side movement to balance the vehicle and quick dismounting, seem set to stay, while others like the 'Equirotal' four-wheeler hinged in the middle to allow the Whip always to face the animals did not become popular. Disc brakes are more powerful than drum brakes and less affected by water. Steel wheels are almost universally used

The Equirotal Carriage built by William Bridges Adams. This had four equal-sized wheels, each hung on springs which were on the same horizontal level. The body was hinged in the centre so that when the driven animal turned, the front half of the vehicle containing the driver followed his track, while the rear half articulated on a central pivot. The builder claimed that this gave the advantage of both large front wheels and a reasonable lock.

for competition, although one manufacturer has had great success with wooden artillery wheels. This system of manufacture, where the wooden spokes are sandwiched between two metal discs at the hub, is stronger and easier to make than the more common type with a wooden stock. Also, the hub is flat and less likely to catch on posts. However, steel wheels are also gaining in popularity for private driving and show vehicles, and certainly give a great feeling of security and reduced maintenance, though usually at the cost of poorer appearance.

Naming Types of Vehicle

To be able to put a name to each vehicle is not always straightforward, as makers sometimes give different names to similar vehicles. There is, however, a simple way of identifying vehicles which will be accurate in the majority of cases. This is by the seating arrangement. A two-wheeled vehicle with two forward-facing seats is a Gig. If a two-wheeler carries back passengers they will usually be seated facing backwards in order to keep their weight over the axle. This vehicle, whether two- or four-wheeled, would be a Dog Cart or its town version, a Ralli Car. The difference between the two lies in the curved sides and dashboard of the Ralli Car compared to the square outline of the Dog Cart. If all passengers in a two-wheeler face inwards, it is a Governess Cart and, if outwards, it is a Jaunting Car. If all the seats in a four-wheeler face forwards it is a Phaeton and if the back passengers face inwards it is a Waggonette or its big cousin, the Body Break. This covers most common vehicles, though there are many variations like the Malvern and Moray Cars, which have the seating position of a Ralli Car but with curved mudguards which follow the wheels for almost half their circumference. There is also the Demi Tonneau (Leicester Car), a form of two-wheeled Waggonette.

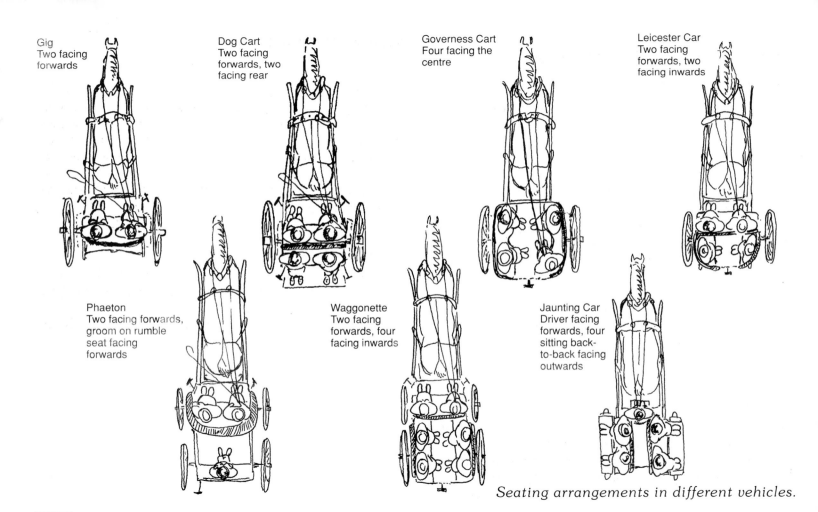

Gig
Two facing
forwards

Dog Cart
Two facing
forwards, two
facing rear

Governess Cart
Four facing the
centre

Leicester Car
Two facing
forwards, two
facing inwards

Phaeton
Two facing forwards,
groom on rumble
seat facing
forwards

Waggonette
Two facing
forwards, four
facing inwards

Jaunting Car
Driver facing
forwards, four
sitting back-
to-back facing
outwards

Seating arrangements in different vehicles.

52

Vehicle Types: Advantages and Disadvantages

Each type of vehicle has its own features which can bring advantages and disadvantages.

Cranked Axles

A cranked axle allows the floor to be kept closer to the ground. This is useful with a Governess Cart as it makes it easier for children to climb in. With a Float, this type of axle makes it easier to load milk churns, livestock or, with a specialised type of Float, horses. These vehicles were used, in town mainly, to collect casualty horses who had collapsed in harness. Cranked axles are now used for some vehicles to be driven by disabled people from their wheelchairs. The main advantage is easy loading, but there is also the good balance and comfort associated with large wheels.

Cab-fronted Vehicles

A cab-fronted vehicle, where the shafts stop at the dashboard, allows easy, low access from in front of the wheels of a two-wheeler. The disadvantage is the extra weight of the shaft mounting brackets, but this design is probably the best when trying to keep the vehicle and its occupants in proportion to a small pony.

Pneumatic Tyres

Wide Pneumatic tyres give a smoother ride than traditional narrow ones and easier draught over soft ground, provided that they don't sink in. If the wheels are going to cut grooves in the ground anyway, then the narrower they are the better. The disadvantage of pneumatic tyres is the risk of punctures and especially burst tyres, which are liable to cause bolting.

Four- and Two-wheelers

Four-wheeled vehicles are more comfortable than two-wheelers, but are more difficult to pull because of their greater weight and increased resistance. They are also unstable on full lock, when they virtually become three-wheelers, if most of the weight is on the front wheels.

CHAPTER 8

Choice of Harness

The choice of harness will be governed by the type of job it is required to do: whether it is to be used by a single animal or by a pair, team or tandem, for show ring work or across country with a two- or four-wheeled carriage. For each purpose the appropriate style of harness is needed and it must also be made from the material best suited.

General Considerations

Fine light Gig harness with patent leather facings would be quickly spoiled if used in cross-country driving, whereas the synthetic webbing and riveted harness would be inappropriate for the show ring. In our modern against-the-clock lifestyle the time it will take to clean and maintain may also be a factor, but safety and comfort of the animal must be of prime importance when the final decision is made.

If a heavy load is to be pulled, the maximum area of shoulder needs to be covered, so a thick, broad collar is used. The same logic applies to the saddle or pad. If only the traces or independent shaft of a four-wheeler need support, a narrow or light pad will serve, but a market-type Cart, Float or Cab will need a more substantial pad, which can still be shaped elegantly.

While a fixed back band is an advantage with a four-wheeled carriage, it can be the cause of injury to the animal, (if not an actual tip-over) when used with a

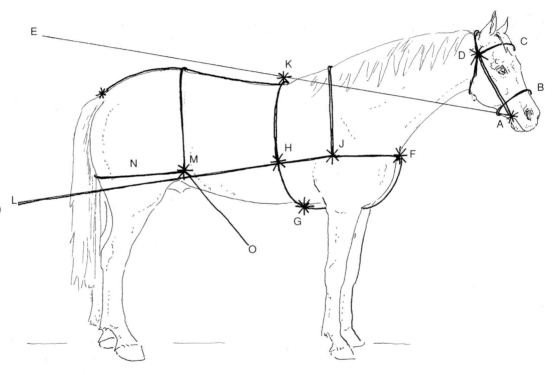

A from corner of mouth over poll to
   same point on opposite side

B loose measurement round nose for
   noseband

C length of browband

D round throat to same point on
   opposite side

E length of rein from bit to buckle

F to G loose measure for length of
   martingale

H for breast collar. Round breast (via F)
   to same point on opposite side

H to J for position of neckstrap in
   relation to tug buckle

K round girth in pad position

L to H for length of trace

M over loin to same point on other side

N round quarters from M to same point
   on other side

O from point M for length of breeching
   strap

Measuring for harness.

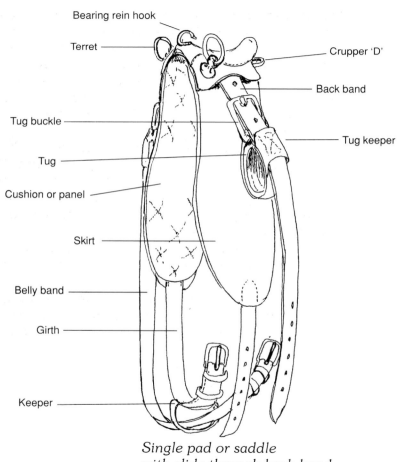

Bearing rein hook

Terret

Crupper 'D'

Back band

Tug buckle

Tug keeper

Tug

Cushion or panel

Skirt

Belly band

Girth

Keeper

*Single pad or saddle
with slide-through back band*

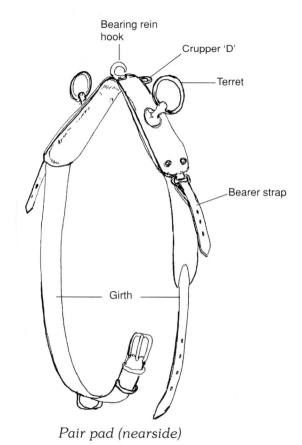

Bearing rein
hook

Crupper 'D'

Terret

Bearer strap

Girth

Pair pad (nearside)

Types of pad or saddle.

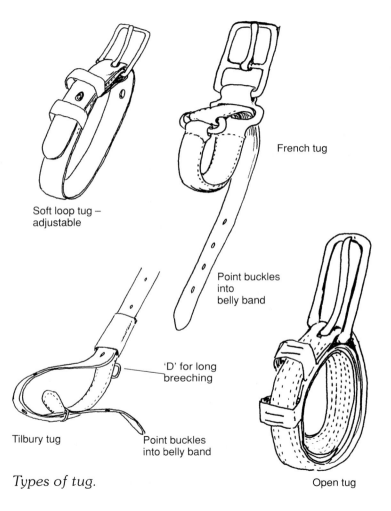

Soft loop tug –
adjustable

French tug

Point buckles
into
belly band

'D' for long
breeching

Tilbury tug

Point buckles
into belly band

Open tug

Types of tug.

two-wheeler on uneven ground. The principle is that a free-running back band makes allowances for any sudden change of height in the shafts – if one wheel strikes a bump the shock can be harmlessly absorbed, rather than knocking the horse off balance. The sliding back band also prevents the pad from being twisted against the side of the animal's spine and allows for fine adjustment when balancing the vehicle.

The traditional tug was of stitched leather and shaped to allow the wooden shaft room for a little play within it. With the thinner metal shaft used on many modern carriages, there is a danger of too much movement and of the tug stop going through the tug, perhaps even catching on the front side. When the animal comes into draught again he is then pulling on the pad. A smaller tug is needed with this type of shaft or alternatively, a soft tug which can be adjusted for size.

Whichever type of crupper dock is chosen, be it a floppy loop or a traditional leather 'formed' one, it must be kept clean and smooth against the soft underskin of the animal's dock.

Trace ends should be used with the type of trace hooks they were designed for.

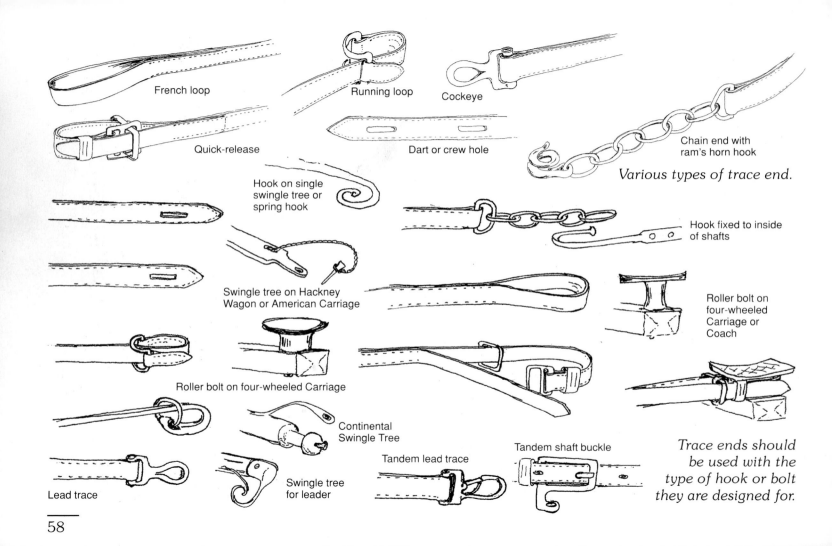

French loop

Running loop

Cockeye

Quick-release

Dart or crew hole

Chain end with ram's horn hook

Various types of trace end.

Hook on single swingle tree or spring hook

Hook fixed to inside of shafts

Swingle tree on Hackney Wagon or American Carriage

Roller bolt on four-wheeled Carriage or Coach

Roller bolt on four-wheeled Carriage

Continental Swingle Tree

Lead trace

Swingle tree for leader

Tandem lead trace

Tandem shaft buckle

Trace ends should be used with the type of hook or bolt they are designed for.

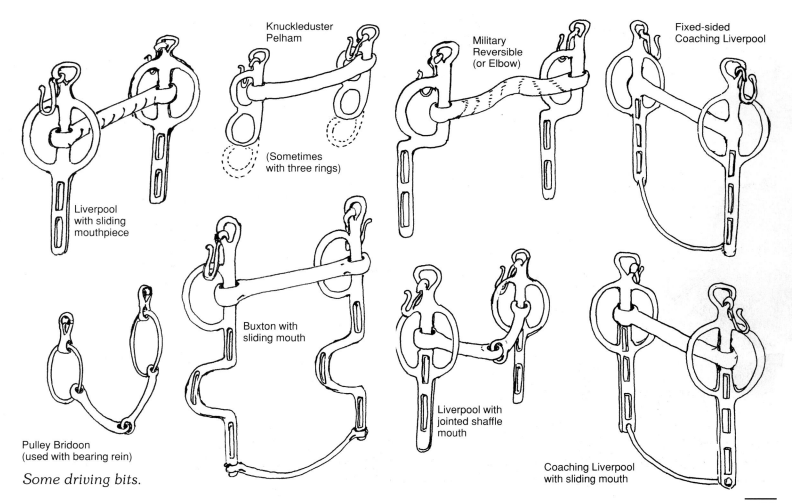

Knuckleduster
Pelham

(Sometimes
with three rings)

Military
Reversible
(or Elbow)

Fixed-sided
Coaching Liverpool

Liverpool
with sliding
mouthpiece

Buxton with
sliding mouth

Liverpool with
jointed shaffle
mouth

Pulley Bridoon
(used with bearing rein)

Some driving bits.

Coaching Liverpool
with sliding mouth

59

The choice of bit will depend upon the magic between the animal's mouth and the Whip's hands. Traditionally, a Wilson snaffle was used with a single trade turnout and for educating a young or 'green' animal, while the family of bits with straight mouthpieces and curbs were used for mature mouths. However well an animal may go in his riding bit there are hidden dangers in using it for driving. For example, a point of a shaft could get caught through it. A specially designed driving bit providing the same action can be found from among this large family of bits.

Collars

The good fit of a collar is essential for a driving animal to be able to work comfortably. The full neck collar must leave the windpipe clear enough to allow you to put your hand between collar and neck while it is lying smoothly back onto the shoulder, and spread the pressure over as large an area as is practicable. The hames should lie level in the groove between the fore wale and after wale, their curve following the same curve as the collar. If this is not so, the rigid hames will quickly pull the collar (made of flexible materials) out of shape and cause the animal's neck to be rubbed. The hame trace pull which makes the line of draught should be positioned where there is the least movement of the shoulder to keep the friction down, although there is bound to be a degree of friction, however well the collar

fits, as each shoulder goes forward in turn. If the trace hooks on the carriage are of the sprung variety or set onto a swingle tree this will help to soften the movement between the animal's neck and the weight of the carriage.

The traditional collar was made of straw, the shape made up and bound and then covered, usually with leather. The lining was also leather, kept clean and soft, although serge or linen linings were generally used for light trade and commercial use. This material, being absorbent, mopped up the sweat and needed drying out each evening and was then thoroughly brushed clean to prevent galling and wringing the shoulders. The fore wale and after wale were covered with leather. Black was the usual colour, patent leather being used for very smart and show wear. Brown was for country use. Polished brown or tan collars with black harness were usual with Road Coaches and also with country and sporting carriages like Mail Phaetons and Dog Carts.

The advantage of a full collar over a breast collar is that the weight is distributed over the whole surface of the shoulder, not just on two small pressure points. For a driving animal to use his maximum strength, the line of draught must pass through his centre of gravity. This can never happen when a breast collar is used, as the line of draught starts too low. However, the disadvantage of a full collar is that it either fits or it doesn't unlike a breast collar which can be adjusted to fit when the horse or pony changes shape in various stages of fitness. Therefore, time

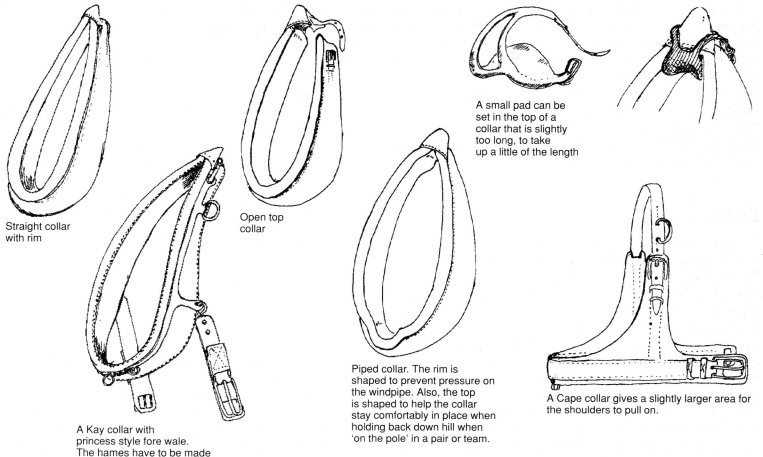

Straight collar
with rim

Open top
collar

A small pad can be
set in the top of a
collar that is slightly
too long, to take
up a little of the length

A Kay collar with
princess style fore wale.
The hames have to be made
to fit the shape of the collar.

Piped collar. The rim is
shaped to prevent pressure on
the windpipe. Also, the top
is shaped to help the collar
stay comfortably in place when
holding back down hill when
'on the pole' in a pair or team.

A Cape collar gives a slightly larger area for
the shoulders to pull on.

Types of collar.

61

and thought must go into fitting the animal with his collar and the hames to the collar. A collar which is too small will put pressure on the windpipe and may actually stop the animal by choking him. One which is too large will rock, pivot and rub up and down causing chafeing, galling and even open sores. The animal will be uncomfortable in his work and jibbing or rearing may be his only defence against the pain. Imagine having to walk long distances in a pair of shoes which do not fit, and you will have some idea of the misery caused by a badly fitting collar.

From this it will be seen that, when buying a collar to fit a particular animal, accurate measurements are needed. This applies whether it is being made specially, or is an off-the-peg one found, perhaps, in a market. The best way to ascertain measurements is to borrow a selection and try them on. When one is found which fits, it can be used by the collar maker to copy, or as a guide when purchasing.

Checking the Fit of the Collar

When the collar is on and pushed back to lie flat on the slope of the shoulders there should be enough room to run two fingers between the neck and the collar along its length. There must also be enough room at the front to grasp the collar at its throat while still leaving clearance for your knuckles. When weight is put on the traces the collar

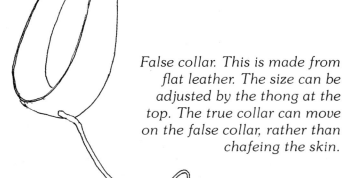

False collar. This is made from flat leather. The size can be adjusted by the thong at the top. The true collar can move on the false collar, rather than chafeing the skin.

Measuring points for a collar.

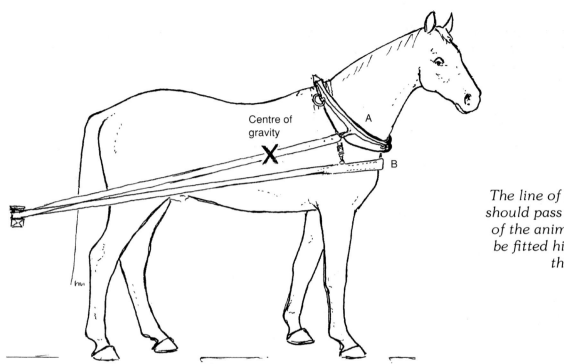

Centre of
gravity

X

A

B

The line of draught from a full collar (A) should pass through the centre of gravity of the animal. A breast collar (B) cannot be fitted high enough to achieve this, so the pulling capacity is reduced.

should not rock either forward or backward, but should lie still.

The next test is to watch from the ground to see whether the collar stays in the same position when the animal is driven at a good trot. A collar which seemed long enough while at the halt may prove too short when the animal is in action, particularly if he has a big crest.

A critical look must then be taken at the height of the tug or anchor pull on the hame. This is to see whether it comes in the best place in conjunction with the height of the trace hooks to make the draught come on the shoulder blades at the part well away from the shoulder joints or point of shoulder, and also to ensure that the draught will pass through the animal's centre of gravity.

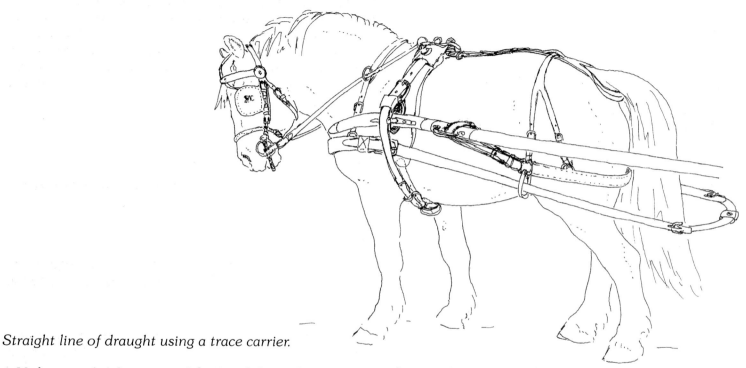

Straight line of draught using a trace carrier.

Unfortunately, the size and fitting of the collar required will vary with circumstance; whether the animal is grass fat, or fit; whether he has his winter or summer coat and with his age. One of the advantages of a breast collar is that it can be made to fit more easily. Also it is cooler in very hot weather, and it flatters a short-necked, cobby type of animal better than a full collar.

The false martingale is buckled around the throat of the collar, or to the front of the hames. It must not pull on the collar, but should come into action when the animal is out of draught and going down hill, when it restrains the collar from bouncing about.

CHAPTER 9

Single Harness: Fitting and Putting To

While being harnessed, the animal should be under control at all times. Once a headcollar or halter has been fitted, he can be either held by an assistant or tied up using a quick-release knot so, should he panic or fall, he can be released immediately. Any dried mud or sweat must be brushed off before harnessing, and the feet should be picked out and shoes checked.

Fitting Single Harness

Always harness up in strict order, starting with the collar.

The Collar

This carries an attachment for the traces, through which the forward movement of the animal is transmitted to the vehicle.

To Fit a Breast Collar. Undo the buckle on the neck strap, reassemble on the animal's neck. The fitting of the collar is most important; the height of the breast piece is altered by adjusting the carrying buckles on the neck strap. If the breast piece is *too low*, the movement of the shoulders will be impaired; if *too high*, the pull will come across the windpipe. Very careful fitting is therefore essential for a happily working and breathing animal.

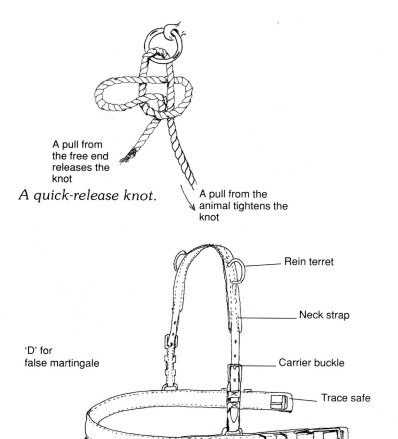

A pull from
the free end
releases the
knot

A quick-release knot.

A pull from the
animal tightens the
knot

Rein terret

Neck strap

'D' for
false martingale

Carrier buckle

Trace safe

Breast collar.

Tug trace buckle

To Fit a Full Collar and Hames Take the collar with the broad part to the top (this shape corresponds to the shape of the animal's head) and put it over the head without putting pressure on the eyes. If necessary, first widen it a little by stretching the collar sideways over your knee. Push the collar down the neck a little way and fit the hames. These are metal attachments for the traces, which sit in the grooves of the collar, thereby distributing the pulling strain over a larger surface than that given by a breast collar.

Having checked that the hames are level, secure them together with the hame strap. Then bring the collar and hames up the neck to just behind the ears and turn the collar the right way up, making sure it is turned the way the mane falls. Next, lift the collar down the neck so that it lies comfortably against the shoulders. There should be room to put your fingers between the animal's neck and the throat of the collar to ensure that no pressure is going to come on the windpipe. (From previous experience it may be known that the collar and hames can be put on comfortably as one unit.)

On a single set of harness, all buckles need to be secured from the nearside of the animal (which is the kerbside of the road). Therefore, the hame strap is carried in the top eye of the offside hame, passed over the top of the collar, through the top eye of the nearside hame, then back through the buckle and is pulled firmly and done up.

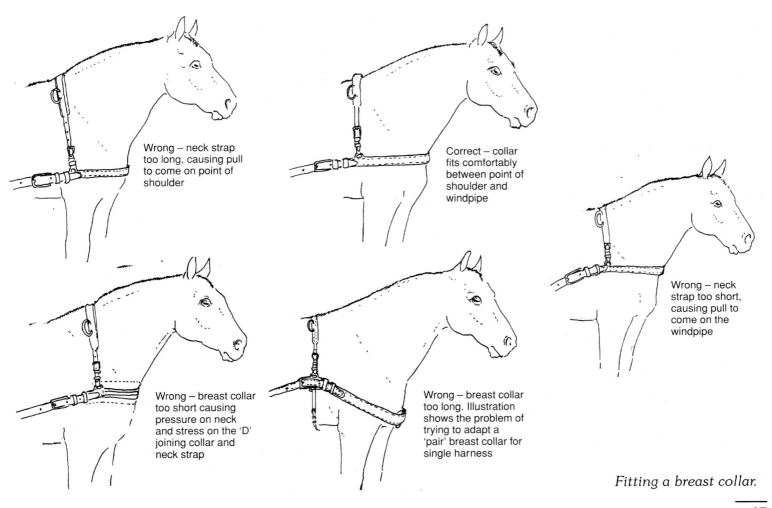

Wrong – neck strap too long, causing pull to come on point of shoulder

Correct – collar fits comfortably between point of shoulder and windpipe

Wrong – neck strap too short, causing pull to come on the windpipe

Wrong – breast collar too short causing pressure on neck and stress on the 'D' joining collar and neck strap

Wrong – breast collar too long. Illustration shows the problem of trying to adapt a 'pair' breast collar for single harness

Fitting a breast collar.

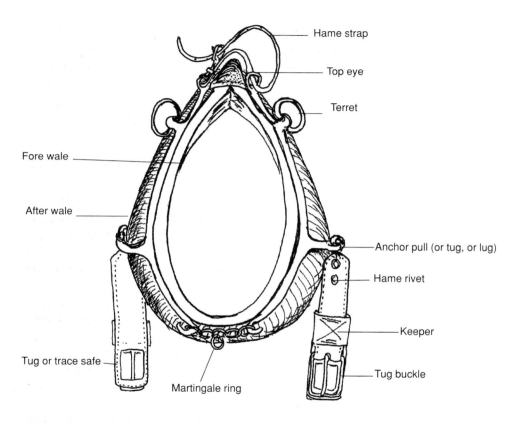

Hame strap

Top eye

Terret

Fore wale

After wale

Anchor pull (or tug, or lug)

Hame rivet

Keeper

Tug or trace safe

Martingale ring

Tug buckle

Full collar with hames.

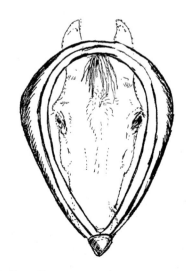

Full collar inverted to pass over head.

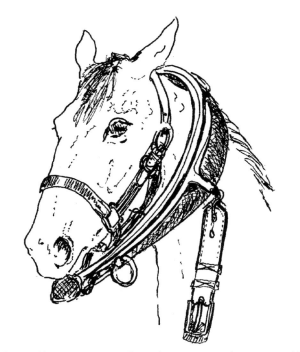

The collar is inverted and put over the animal's head before turning it in the same direction as the mane lies.

The False Martingale. This is not essential for single driving, though it may help to keep the collar from bouncing about. When fitted, it is buckled to the ring or 'D' at the front of the collar; if none is provided, pass the billet round the front of the collar and buckle it up. The other end hangs ready for the girth to be passed through it.

The Traces. These connect the collar to the vehicle, thereby transmitting the horsepower to the vehicle. The trace threads through the trace safe, then through the tug buckle, with the point of the trace pushed tidily home through the keepers. A loose knot can then be tied in the traces to keep them off the ground temporarily.

The Pad or Saddle, Back Band and Tugs, Back Strap and Crupper

The back band threads through the pad and carries the tugs, which carry the shafts. Through the tugs, the weight of the vehicle is distributed via the back band to the pad, and thus spread upon the animal's back and barrel. The pad has a channel up the centre to prevent damage to the spine.

Place the pad onto the animal's back with the crupper 'D' towards the tail. Check that the girths are not twisted and that they hang just behind the elbow. If using a martingale, thread the girth through its loop, then do the girth up tightly enough to prevent the pad from sliding round. Do up the belly band, leaving plenty of slack so that the tugs may lie freely on the panel of the pad.

The back strap and crupper are to prevent the pad from going forward; thread the back strap through the 'D' at the rear of the pad and do it up on the longest hole, lying the strap along the animal's back. Stroke the animal along his back, take hold of his dock and lift the tail sideways away from the quarters, folding the long hairs up and under to enable the whole tail to be passed comfortably and quickly through the crupper. Slide the crupper up as far as it will go, checking that it is comfortable with no hairs caught, then gently let go of the dock, keeping tension on the crupper by holding the back strap. Next, adjust the buckle so that it holds the crupper dock against the tail without putting constant pressure on either the tail or the pad. Pass the end point through the keepers.

On some sets of harness, the crupper dock has buckles fitted on it, so that one can be undone and the crupper slid gently and easily under the animal's dock before being rebuckled.

As experience is gained in putting on the crupper, pad and breeching, it may all be put on as one unit, by laying the pad over the back a little to the rear of its final position, lifting it forward after the crupper is in place and then doing up the girth and belly band. As there is little sideways pull on the pad, the girth does not need to be as tight as a riding girth, but a loose girth will rub and cause a girth gall. Therefore, ensure that the skin is not wrinkled by drawing first one foreleg forward, then the other.

The Breeching

The breeching prevents the vehicle running onto the animal when stopping and, through this, he also holds the vehicle back when going down a hill.

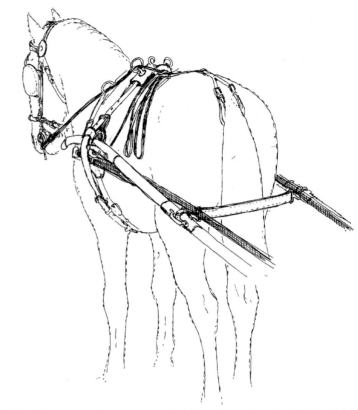

A false breeching is not attached to the animal, but buckled through the 'D' fittings on the shafts. Because of the shape of some shafts, it is not always possible to get the false breeching in the right place but here, it is correctly placed.

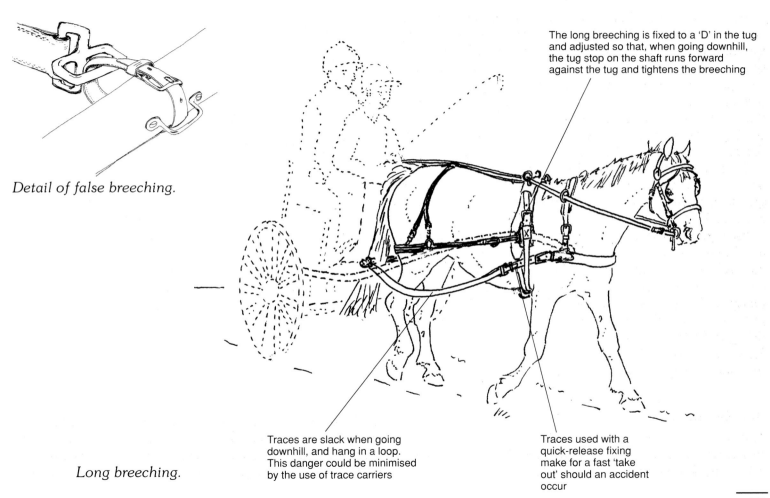

Detail of false breeching.

Long breeching.

The long breeching is fixed to a 'D' in the tug and adjusted so that, when going downhill, the tug stop on the shaft runs forward against the tug and tightens the breeching

Traces are slack when going downhill, and hang in a loop. This danger could be minimised by the use of trace carriers

Traces used with a quick-release fixing make for a fast 'take out' should an accident occur

Full Breeching If this is being used, thread the loin strap through the back strap in the space provided, so that it is lying just behind the point of hip. Adjust the buckles on the loin strap to allow the seat of breeching to hang level with the stifle joint (halfway from the tail to the hock).

False Breeching A false breeching is not attached to the animal. It is buckled through the 'D' fittings on the shafts, fixed on their exterior faces and situated slightly behind the animal. When fitted the false breeching must not touch the animal when moving forward, but must be close enough to come into contact with the quarters when going downhill or stopping.

Long breeching. This is fixed to a 'D' in the tug and adjusted so that, when going downhill, the tug stop on the shaft runs forward against the tug and tightens the breeching.

The Reins

Through these, contact is kept between the animal's mouth and the Whip's hands. Some reins are made stitched together, in which case sides for fitting are immaterial. If the reins are separate and made to be joined together with a small buckle, this is stitched on the offside rein.

Take the reins and lay them across the animal's back; thread the billet buckle through the terret on the pad and continue straight through the next one on the collar, leaving enough slack to reach the animal's mouth. Repeat with the second rein on the other side. The long ends must now be put up safely onto the pad. This can be done by doubling them and passing them through a terret from the back towards the front. Alternatively, they may be put through the back strap. The idea is to prevent the long ends from trailing on the ground, and to have them up so that they will come smoothly and instantly to hand when required.

The Bridle

The bridle is the means of carrying the bit in the animal's mouth and supporting the winkers (also known as blinkers or blinders). Before fitting the bridle, the headcollar can be removed and buckled around the top of the neck. Check that the forelock is lying smoothly forward and the mane back. Then take the bridle in the left hand, checking that the noseband, throatlash and curb chain are undone. Place the right hand over the animal's head and transfer the headpiece into it. With the index finger of the left hand supporting the bit, insert the thumb into the corner of the animal's mouth; slight pressure on the bars should cause the jaws to open. Immediately slide the bit into the mouth and at the same time draw the headpiece back and hold it there. The ears will pop through the spaces between the browband, winker stay and headpiece. Slide your finger

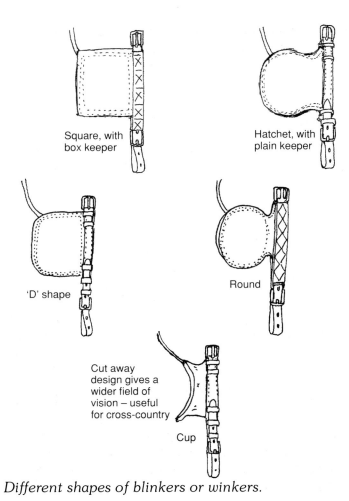

Square, with
box keeper

Hatchet, with
plain keeper

'D' shape

Round

Cut away
design gives a
wider field of
vision – useful
for cross-country

Cup

Different shapes of blinkers or winkers.

under the bridle headpiece and make sure that the mane and forelock are smooth and comfortable. Check that the bridle is well back on the head.

By altering the top buckle on the cheek strap, the winkers can be raised or lowered, so that the eye is covered by the centre of the winker. The width between them is controlled by the buckle on the poll. The height of the bit is adjusted by the buckles below the winkers. The bit acts on the bars of the mouth and should be fitted in the mouth so that it neither pulls the corners up nor hangs down and interferes with the front teeth. However, some animals go best when the bit is high enough to cause one or two wrinkles at the sides of the mouth. If the bit is fitted so low that the tongue comes over it, control can be lost and an accident ensue. If a curb bit is being used, the curb chain is turned so that all the links lie flat before being done up.

The throatlash is done up tight enough to prevent the bridle from slipping off, but loose enough to allow the animal to flex (when he drops his nose and relaxes his jaw, the muscles at the top of his neck expand). The noseband keeps the bridle close against the head, preventing the animal from seeing behind and under the winkers. It also prevents the mouth opening wide enough to evade the bit, but should not be uncomfortably tight (allow room to insert one finger between the lower jawbone and the noseband).

Finally, the position of the reins is selected and they are buckled on to the bit. The headcollar is then removed and the animal is ready to put to.

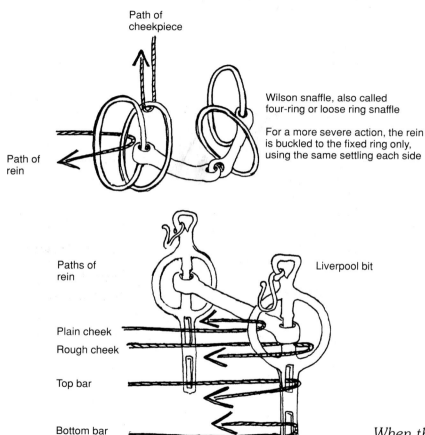

Path of
cheekpiece

Wilson snaffle, also called
four-ring or loose ring snaffle

For a more severe action, the rein
is buckled to the fixed ring only,
using the same settling each side

Path of
rein

Paths of
rein

Liverpool bit

Plain cheek

Rough cheek

Top bar

Bottom bar

Examples of rein attachments for driving bits.

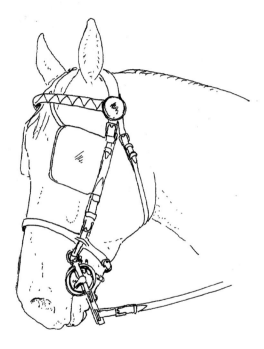

*When the rein is attached to the bottom bar of a bit
such as a Liverpool bit, severe pressure is transmitted
to the bars of the mouth, poll and lower jaw.*

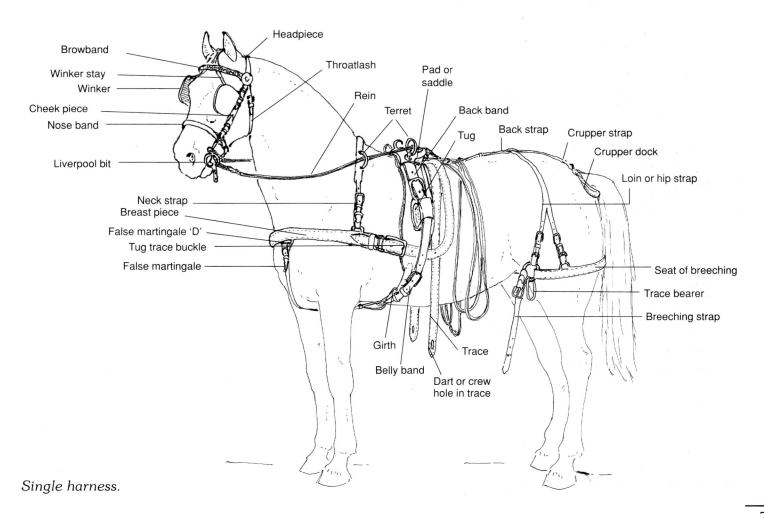

Single harness.

Browband

Winker stay

Winker

Cheek piece

Nose band

Liverpool bit

Headpiece

Throatlash

Rein

Terret

Pad or saddle

Back band

Tug

Back strap

Crupper strap

Crupper dock

Loin or hip strap

Neck strap

Breast piece

False martingale 'D'

Tug trace buckle

False martingale

Girth

Belly band

Dart or crew hole in trace

Trace

Seat of breeching

Trace bearer

Breeching strap

Preparing to Put To

Having harnessed the animal, the next step is to lead him to the vehicle. Remember that, with his winkers on, he cannot see behind. He relies entirely on you to take care that he does not get hurt or surprised by getting caught up or bumped. For example, on leaving the stable (if you have to bridle him in the stable) open the door wide and fasten it back. The handler should turn and walk backwards with a hand either side of the bit so that the animal is guided steadily through the centre of the doorway. When leading the animal, a watch must be kept to prevent the traces and reins from falling down.

The vehicle should be standing ready in a clear area with its cushions, knee rugs, lamps, whip, gloves, etc. already in it, together with your spares kit. If using a false breeching, this should also have been fitted in place. Alternatively, to shorten the time that the animal has to stand before moving off, the Whip can already have put on hat, coat and knee apron, one corner of which can be tucked up into the waistband to keep it well clear of the feet. If gloves are not worn while putting to they can also be handily tucked into the waistband.

Putting To

Stand the animal in a straight line a little in front of the shafts. An assistant should stand in front of him holding his head, hands either side of the bit on the reins.

The animal should be put to as quickly as possible. To reduce the danger time of his being half in and half out, prepare the traces so that they can go quickly onto the trace hooks. To do this, undo the knots and pass the traces between the pad and the belly band, then lay them over the back. If trace carriers are being used, pass the traces through them. Check that the belly band is slack enough to allow the shafts through the tugs. Now lift the shafts high and pull the vehicle up to the animal, speaking all the while, so that he knows what is happening. Lower the shafts carefully, placing the points into the tugs and pull the vehicle up until the stops come against the tugs. Quickly put the trace onto the trace hook. To do this, pull the vehicle up towards the animal with one hand, shortening the distance to get the trace onto the hook, turning the trace towards you so that there will be no twist when it is on. Go round to the other side and repeat with the second trace. To fasten the breeching strap, pass it under the trace and then the shaft, up through the shaft 'D' and buckle it up. Alternatively, the trace may lie over the breeching strap if this allows it to run in a straighter line. Go round to the other side and fasten the other breeching strap in the

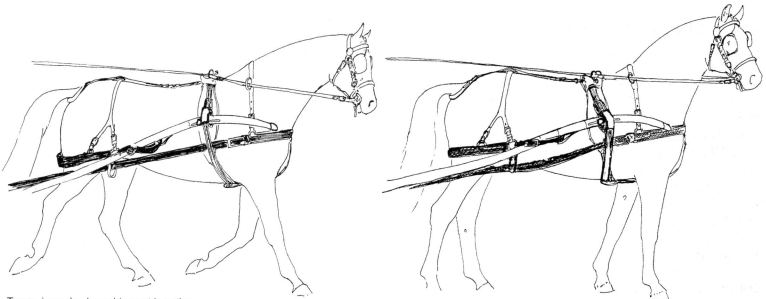

Traces in work – breeching not in action

The adjustment of traces and breeching.

Traces slack, breeching in action, tug stops against the tugs, pushing them forward thus taking a little weight on the back

same way. If a trace carrier is being used, there is no need to carry the trace with the breeching strap. Tighten the belly band and check the girth, then walk round and double check that everything is correctly fitted and safely fastened.

When a breast collar is used, the trace hooks should be sprung or set onto a swingle tree. This softens the action

between the animal's shoulder and the vehicle, reduces the risk of galling, and thus makes it both easier on the animal and more comfortable for those riding in the carriage.

Checking Balance of a Two-wheeled Vehicle

When a two-wheeled vehicle is loaded, and the belly band

adjusted, the shafts should almost float within the tugs. There are several holes in the back band for the alteration of the height of the tugs and the back band is made to slide through the pad to keep the tugs level. When the animal moves forward, and the traces are tight, the tug stop should still be against the tug with the tug falling naturally in the centre of the pad. The trace is too long if animal and pad move forward, and too short if the tug is forced in front of the pad while the animal is moving forward.

The breeching must not come into play while the animal is standing on the level, nor while moving forward, but the moment he stops, the weight of the vehicle will push the tug forward slightly with the tug stops and the weight will be distributed onto the animal's back. The breeching should come into use at this point. When going downhill, the breeching will be in strong contact with the quarters, allowing the animal to hold the vehicle back. If the breeching is fitted too high it will be uncomfortable and may cause him to kick. If fitted too low it can prevent the hind legs from working properly and even push them away under him and cause a fall.

Taking Out

When taking the animal out of the vehicle the reverse procedure from putting to should be followed strictly. The assistant stands in front of the animal, holding the reins close to the bit, one hand each side. The long ends of the reins can then be put up on the pad. If using a full breeching, undo the breeching strap, taking it out of the 'D', and let it hang free. Go round to the other side and undo the breeching strap there. Pull the vehicle up a little toward the animal to allow enough slack to be able to unhook and remove the trace from the trace hook. The free trace must not be allowed to trail on the floor, so either a knot can be tied in it or it can be laid over the animal's back, but make sure that it is well forward and over enough not to fall down. Go quickly to the other side and repeat the procedure. Next, making sure that the loop of the reins is hanging in front of the tug stop, slacken the belly band enough to allow the tugs to free the shafts. Next, take hold of the shaft and push the vehicle back until it is clear of the animal. The points of the shafts can rest temporarily on the ground.

Lead the animal away, remembering that with his winkered bridle he cannot see behind. To secure the animal for safety, take the headcollar and buckle it round his neck and tie him up. Alternatively, if a headcollar with a buckle on the noseband is used, it can be put on properly under the bridle by means of this buckle before the bridle is removed.

Unharnessing

This is done in the reverse order from harnessing up.

The Bridle. To remove the bridle, undo the reins from the bit. The throatlash, noseband and curb chain should all be undone. Take hold of the headpiece and gently pull the bridle forward and down. Keep hold of the animal with your arm on his neck until he has released the bit from his mouth. Put the headcollar on properly and tie him up.

The Reins. Pull these back through the rings and terrets, fold them tidily and place them with the bridle at a safe distance from the animal.

The Pad. Undo the belly band and girth, free the martingale and slide the pad back a little to allow the crupper to be slid down the tail. Hold the dock away from the quarters while this is done. Lift the pad, back strap, crupper and breeching back and away, all as one unit. (With some animals, especially those with a full tail, it may be best to unbuckle the crupper dock – in which case the girth and belly band can be undone after the crupper is removed.)

Breast Collar and Traces. These can be removed together, either by unbuckling the neckstrap or by turning the whole thing over, going the way the mane lies and slipping over the head.

Full Collar and Hames. Bring the collar up the neck and turn it over, going the way the mane lies. If the collar was broad enough to go on with the hames fitted, bring it straight over the head, being careful not to snag the lining on the headcollar buckle. If the collar was tight against the animal's eyes when being put on, then the hames must be removed before taking off the collar.

Variations in Harness and Harnessing
Four-wheeled Vehicles with Independent Shafts

When using a four-wheeled carriage that has shafts which are independent from each other, a different type of tug is used – the Tilbury (or French). These grip the shafts, usually between a pair of stops. To keep the shafts close against the animal, there is a keeper stitched to the skirt of the pad through which the belly band passes. With this arrangement, the traces cannot go between the pad and belly band, but are passed over the outer side of the belly band. The breeching can then work in the usual way as the shafts are held firmly, preventing them rising as the breeching comes into work. If the shafts did rise the vehicle would run onto the animal, causing all kinds of undesirable events!

As the shafts are independent, there is a danger that one shaft may slide down and the other up if a pad with a freely sliding back band is used.

Harness for Donkeys and Mules

The proportions of a donkey or mule are very different from those of a pony. For example a donkey's head is generally larger in proportion to the size of his body than is the case with a pony. Therefore, alterations to the following will be necessary to make a set of pony harness fit:

The Bridle. The browband will need to be longer (probably cob size) as it is most important that the bridle goes right back on the head and far enough down so that there is no pressure on the base of the ears.

The Collar. With a breast collar the distance around the breast between the neckstrap 'D's may be shorter.

A full collar which would fit the donkey's shoulder will not be able to pass over his head as the donkey's shoulders are much smaller in comparison than a pony's. Therefore, an open top collar must be used. The top of the collar is opened up, placed around the neck and firmly closed again before putting on the hames.

Pad and Breeching. Provided that the girth and belly band are the right length, the pad should be satisfactory. Shetland size will look right but anything larger will probably swamp the animal.

Donkeys have longer backs and smaller quarters than ponies, so alterations in the back strap and breeching will be needed.

Bearing Reins ('Top' or 'Overcheck' Reins)

Anna Sewell, the author of *Black Beauty*, depicted the cruelty of badly and inconsiderately fitted bearing reins most graphically. The pain inflicted by the forcing of animals' heads unnaturally high in the 'fashion' of the day was most horrible. A driving animal needs to lower his head in order to use his back muscles to start a heavy load and pull it uphill. However a properly fitted bearing rein is not cruel when used with lightweight carriages on the flat and is often seen in the show ring, particularly with Hackneys.

When a horse holds his head nicely in a good position, there is good contact between the curb bit and the Whip's hand but, if he lowers his head to pull and bore, the bearing rein comes into action, taking some of the weight and making a lighter and more pleasant drive. It also encourages the animal to use his haunches and hocks by bringing them more underneath him. It is true that the bearing rein can be said to be a false aid, since an animal can acquire obedience with a light mouth and plenty of impulsion through schooling. However, its use can be considered correct with traditional harness; a Hackney or team put to a Park Drag, or with a ladies' carriage.

If exercising a pony who is kept a bit hungry to help prevent laminitis, a variation of the bearing rein can be used to prevent him from putting his head down to snatch for grass.

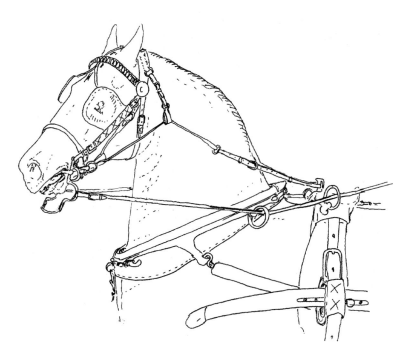

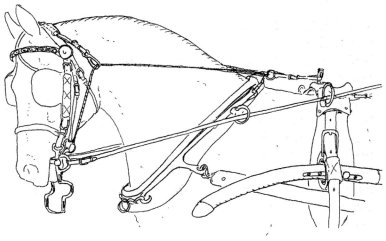

An unkindly fitted bearing rein, forcing the head up and back.

A bearing rein fitted to a separate bridoon helps to establish and maintain correct head carriage. Correctly adjusted, it only comes into action when the head is lowered. It should be released from the hook on the pad when the animal is to be allowed to stand relaxed.

CHAPTER 10

How to Drive in Single Harness

Driving an equine is very different from riding. Having said that, the person who can both ride and drive is a far more complete horseman or horsewoman than the one who specialises in one or the other. There are still some people who preach that riding animals should only be ridden and driving animals only driven but, if your animal is capable of doing both and you are too, then far more mutual understanding and respect can be developed, and there will be a lovely feeling of completeness.

Regular riding, interspersed with long-reining, make a change from driving and will help alleviate boredom, especially for the fully stabled animal.

If you are unable to ride yourself, it is usually possible to find someone who will ride for you but, do remember, it is most important that they use the same word commands as you do when driving. If you can school your animal to movements on command from the saddle, all the better.

Changes in Technique

The technique of driving has had to change over the years, because of the ever-changing pattern of transport in general, the continual regrading of our roads and lanes, new legislation and general public opinion.

It is a sad fact of life that the vast majority of people have forgotten that equines were, until well into the twentieth century, our main form of transport. The first recorded date of wheeled vehicles drawn by four onager stallions was around 4000 BC, which makes the present internal combustion automobile still a very junior means of transport. However, even though the harness animal is the senior citizen of transport, it is important that we maintain courtesy to all other road users and produce and drive our animals in a safe and controllable manner. This means that, not only do the animals have to be schooled correctly, but we, the humans in charge of the safety angle, must be able to drive in a manner which accords with present day traffic and will not cause danger or annoyance. In addition to being a matter of consideration of other road users this will minimise the prospect of any legislation which might reduce the scope for driving.

In the days gone by, it was considered correct to drive with a rein in each hand, so balancing the animal. There were clear, open roads and tracks with very few motorised vehicles of any description. If driven animals did 'take off' (bolt) unexpectedly, there was little likelihood of making contact with another vehicle. Yes, the coach might have ended up in a ditch, but in general there would not have been the wholesale disasters which can occur nowadays. Also, in the old days, if the animals decided something was dangerous and spooked, the full width of the road was often available so again, there was less chance of a catastrophe. It didn't matter so much if the driving whip was not immediately to hand to help correct the animals back onto their correct line of travel.

In contrast, a drawback to driving with a rein in each hand nowadays is that, should you have to do an emergency stop, it is so easy to 'run out of leather'. If, however, the reins are held as described below, you can shorten them immediately and stop safely – and you are, in any case, more likely to remain in control. Furthermore, if your animal spooks and your whip is already in your right hand, there is no time lost in using it to correct the line of travel.

In this and other respects the British Driving Society remains aware of the changing conditions pertinent to the driving of all equines and regularly updates the guidelines for safe and courteous driving. The driving technique described below has been accepted by the BDS as encouraging safety and control, and their tests are based upon it.

Preparing to Drive

Once the animal has been put to and the groom is still holding his head (or is positioned where he can steady him), put on your gloves, tuck the corner of the driving apron up into the waist and make sure your hat is on securely and will not blow off. Do a quick final check of everything. It is the Whip's responsibility to ensure everything is fitting correctly; all buckles done up, all straps in their keepers; the vehicle safe and balanced and spares to hand.

Mounting the Vehicle

It is correct to mount from either side of all vehicles, except for trade vehicles, which are always mounted from the nearside and Coaches, which are always mounted from the offside.

Nearside (kerb side) Mounting. Place the whip against the seat on the right side of the vehicle. Pick up the reins and hold them in the driving position in your left hand, keeping a light but definite contact on the animal's mouth. Too firm a contact will encourage your animal to start reversing, which is extremely dangerous. Put the spare length of reins over your left arm or hook them up on the little finger of your left hand. Hold the dashboard handle with the thumb and first two fingers of your left hand. Next, take the handle near the seat in your right hand and, using the steps on the vehicle, get up. Move straight over to the offside as quickly and smoothly as possible and sit down. Drop the corner of the apron, pick up the whip in your right hand and immediately assume the driving position and be ready to drive.

Offside Mounting. This is not quite the same as mounting from the nearside. The whip is placed against the seat in the middle of the vehicle, you get up with the reins in your right hand (again with the contact on the mouth of the animal) and the spare rein over the right arm *but* instead of the reins being held with the two top fingers between them, you drop each rein down one finger. This allows you to use the index or first finger in conjunction with the thumb to hold the dashboard handle while getting up (the left hand holding the handle by the seat). Sit down quickly, immediately transfer the reins to the left hand in the driving position, drop the corner of the apron, pick up the whip with the right hand and be ready to drive.

Dismounting

Always dismount backwards, never get out of the vehicle facing forwards and never dismount before your groom or passengers. If the animal should suddenly decide to move off, you need to be able to spring back into the vehicle and be in control. If you are facing away from the vehicle and the animal moves away, you will end up on your nose and lose control of the turnout.

Nearside Dismounting. Lay the whip against the seat on your offside, tuck up your apron, put the spare rein over your left arm and shorten up your reins so that as you stand up and take the dashboard handle in your right hand, you still have the animal on the bit. Steady yourself with your right hand on the other handle and step down backwards, saying quietly but firmly to your animal 'Stand'. Still keeping a very light contact on the bit, fold the reins in the approved manner and place them through the terret. You can then commence the taking out procedure.

Offside Dismounting. Put the whip in the middle of the vehicle against the seat. (It is considered incorrect to put the whip in the whip holder because, all too frequently, good whips have been broken while vehicles were being put away. Also, if the whip is in the holder when driving, an accident can easily have happened during the second or two it takes to get it out for use.) Next, turn up a corner of the apron into the waist, transfer the reins to the right hand (holding them in the same manner as for mounting) and go down backwards, keeping the animal just on the bit and giving the command 'Stand'. Hang up the reins in the approved manner and commence the taking out procedure.

The Art of Driving

Neat, tidy hands, good leg and back position, a calm, firm, well-projected voice, a sharp ear and keen eye are the main requisites for driving. Perhaps the most important of these are light hands which can keep a firm but gentle feeling on the bit, and a keen sense of anticipation. Once you have given the nod to your groom to come up beside you, it is you who should be in command, not the animal.

Always, if possible, start the driving session at walk. If he has learnt in the early days of training to move off at trot, it becomes very difficult to persuade the average equine to start off calmly at walk. Remember, when you give the command 'Walk on', to give just very slightly with your wrist for a half second or so; just enough time to allow the animal to start walking on freely, but no so much that you lose contact with his mouth. Then collect him up, after which your hands should be held neatly in front of you at all times.

The Use of the Hands

The Left Hand holds both reins in single, pair, tandem and team driving. It is basically the accelerator, with a measure of steerage control.

As a guide, the left hand should be held about 6–9 cm (2½–3⅓ in) in front of the stomach, just above your navel, the wrist rounded as though you were about to deliver a backhand volley in tennis, or ready to pull a pocket watch out of a pocket in your waistcoat. The back of the hand should be facing the rump of the animal, very slightly rolled towards you, so that you can see only your index finger and thumb, or so that you can just see the stitching on the second knuckle of your glove. The elbow should be comfortably close to your hip bone with the upper arm nearly vertical, which should allow your left wrist to flex gently with the movement of your animal's head. It should be possible to feel, in the tendons of your fingers, the pressure of the bit on the bars of the animal's mouth.

The bottom two fingers of the left hand should hold the reins firmly; it should not be possible to pull the reins out of the left hand if these fingers are working correctly. The top two fingers and thumb should be relaxed except when they are required to assist in certain steering functions, such as looping in tandem and team work (these techniques are discussed in Driving Tandem, Chapter 12).

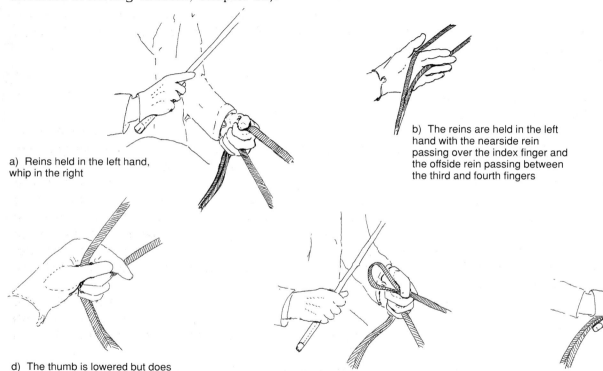

a) Reins held in the left hand, whip in the right

b) The reins are held in the left hand with the nearside rein passing over the index finger and the offside rein passing between the third and fourth fingers

c) The lower fingers curl round the two reins gripping them firmly

d) The thumb is lowered but does not grip the rein because. . .

e) . . . it needs to be free to pinch the rein when taking a loop to turn to the left, or to place the whip under when the right hand has to be empty for making a hand signal – or receiving a rosette!

f) The right hand assisting the left in holding the whip balanced. The middle fingers remain mobile to grasp one or other of the reins (or both) in an emergency stop, or while shortening the reins

The use of the hands.

The Right Hand is held just in front of the left, in such a manner that the index finger and thumb (holding the whip) are just above the left rein.

The right hand has an extremely important part to play. It should be available to use the whip at a split second's notice to help prevent an accident as well as giving road signals to other traffic and assisting with balancing the animal on the bit when steering.

Ideally the index finger and thumb, with the help of the second finger, control the whip, especially the angle at which it is held. The bottom two fingers should be in light contact with the right rein, so as to balance the contact with the animal's mouth.

Ideally, the hands work together, completing sharp left and right turns, emergency halts and driving up and down hills without appearing, to those situated on the ground, to move a great deal.

This method of driving, if executed correctly, has the same effect on the mouth and balance of the animal as does the system of driving with a rein in each hand, but is so very much safer in times of emergency and when signalling to other traffic.

Shortening the Reins

One of the most important rules of safe driving is to make sure you do not take the left hand off the reins. To shorten either, pull the rein tighter from behind the left hand with the right hand, or put the right hand in front of the left hand, hold the rein with the right hand and slide the left hand up the reins without taking them from between the fingers. This is by far the safest way to shorten the reins.

Emergency Stops

To perform an emergency stop, quickly put the right hand well in front of the left on the reins, press firmly downwards and backwards and at the same time push your feet hard forward. Sit well back, give a firm command; 'Whoa' and, at the same time, lift the reins upward with your left hand, pulling it slightly towards your body. The effect is to shorten the reins very quickly and sharply. Practise this on your driving machine (see Off-vehicle practise) because, even though he needs to learn about such things, it is hard on the animal.

It is because emergency stops are needed in this day and age that it is so important to have the bit and curb chain correctly set, so that the curb chain can work if it is needed.

Essentially the same technique can be used, with far less ferocity, when going down a slight hill.

Do remember, it is important to have your animal balanced on the mouth at all times. Emergency stops aside, good, kind hands with supple wrists keep an animal's mouth soft and encourage him to trust and obey.

The Voice

For driving, the voice is an essential aid. The basic voice commands are 'Walk on', 'Trot on', Whoa', 'Steady', 'Stand' and 'Get back'. The two beginning with 'S' are very important words for a horse to learn, especially 'Stand' in emergencies, such as when a piece of harness breaks, or after an accident when you need the animal to remain immobile while things are sorted out. In fact, the word 'Stand' can be used even when an animal is down since, to them, it means 'Don't move'. If an animal understands this it is possible, even in adverse conditions, to remove harness or do whatever is needed to sort out trouble.

Of course, the voice has uses other than in emergencies. It can help with smoother transitions from one gait to another if you catch the animal's attention before giving the command of the 'gear' you wish to go to, so say 'Good boy' or 'Tommy' (whatever the name is), then give your command; 'Trot on' or whatever. A command suddenly bawled out to a horse, pony or donkey can slightly startle them and cause a rough jerky change of movement.

Control of voice projection is an important factor which can easily be overlooked. When driving, the animal's ears are much further in front of you than when riding so, unless a firm, strong command is given, the animal just doesn't hear fully what is being asked. Women especially tend to be too gentle and soft with their voices or else tend to raise their voices when they try to project forwards. The latter can have unfortunate consequences because, if the command comes out to the ears of the animal as a high-pitched squeak, it can sound like human fear and cause the animal to get worried and start panicking. It is well to practise using a full voice, when alone, dropping the pitch and using the vowels in a full, strong manner; 'WAAALK ON', 'TROOOT ON' etc. Shouting is unnecessary.

Finally, remember that all animals like to be praised; it gives them confidence and a feeling of well-being. However, do not use non-stop chatter. This just causes confusion.

The Whip

As stated earlier, the driving whip replaces the rider's leg as an aid to help keep the turnout going where required. When applied quickly and accurately, it can help prevent sudden, dangerous, swerves on the road. The length of the whip and lash in total should be suitable for the size of the animal being driven, so that a flick of the lash lands between the pad and the collar. If used on the quarters, it may provoke kicking, especially with a young or novice animal.

When an animal is being naughty, one sometimes sees the whip applied as a sharp reprimand. This can be a good practice, as long as it is not done too frequently. Usually, horses, ponies and donkeys will soon learn when they are being naughty just from the tone of the Whip's voice.

In addition to its corrective uses the whip can, if held at the correct angle, add elegance to the turnout in the show ring.

Off-vehicle Practise

The secret of good driving is to practise and practise, and this is where a 'driving machine' can be of great use. It is an excellent way of practising correct hand work and perfecting light, sensitive control. The simplest way of setting up such a 'machine' at home is illustrated. Lighter weights can be used instead of horseshoes, although shoes from a donkey or Shetland would be light enough!

Another way of practising is to attach the reins to handles on separate top drawers of a chest, and it is possible to set up quite elaborate devices using pulleys and weights. The less mechanically minded can start practising with long dog leads, and a garden cane to replace the whip!

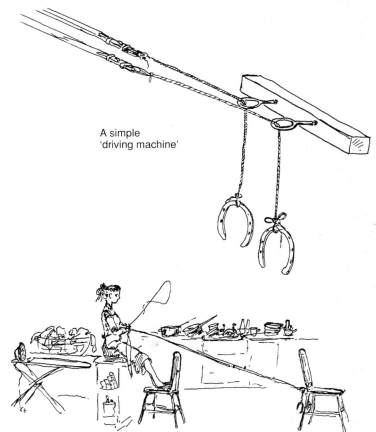

A simple 'driving machine'

Never mind the ironing or washing up – practise!

Off-vehicle practise.

Crouch position –
uncomfortable but
safe for scurry
and short periods

Uncomfortable
and insecure

Awkward and less
secure than good
position

Good, strong comfortable
position

Old-fashioned style for
a coachmen – insecure

Movable foot rest

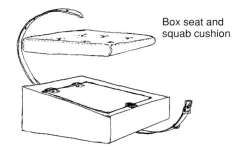

Box seat and
squab cushion

Dumpy or dumpling cushion
used by the coachman on
a Road Coach, Drag or
high sporting Carriage

Driving positions.

Features of the box seat.

Driving position suitable only for scurry, where it is sustained for just a minute or so.

A few minutes practise each day can help a beginner to develop flexible hands and wrists and become used to the movements required for driving. So often, when driving, a novice Whip is tense and shoulders and back soon begin to ache. Regular practise will help to reduce this.

It is worth remembering to sit properly as shown in the illustration 'Driving positions'. The easiest way to think of this seat if you are (or have been) a rider, is to sit as for sitting trot – sit into your pelvis; any movement is above the waist. If you are not a rider, imagine you are sitting in a fast, open-top sports car. Sitting too far forward has been described by the BDS Patron, HRH Prince Philip, as 'sitting on the loo seat'! This seat can be dangerous, because if an animal rears and then plunges forward, the Whip is far more likely to be catapulted over the dashboard than if he or she were sitting correctly, with back straight, thighs sloping and feet at the correct angle.

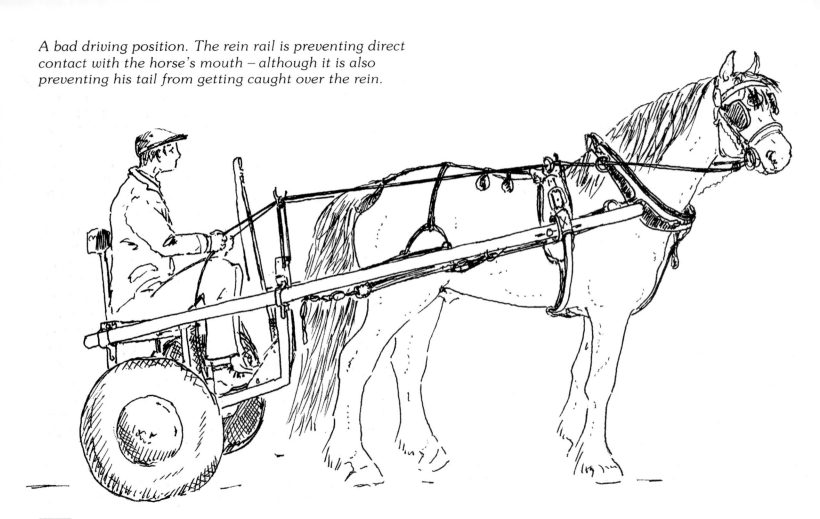

A bad driving position. The rein rail is preventing direct contact with the horse's mouth – although it is also preventing his tail from getting caught over the rein.

CHAPTER 11

Driving Pairs

It is as well to point out from the start that there are certain disadvantages to driving pairs – mainly of a financial nature! The capital outlay is considerably more than for a single animal, especially if purchasing a pair who are proven to go well together. It will also be apparent that the ongoing costs (in both time and money) associated with horsekeeping will be increased considerably, and there are also certain 'hidden extras'. If, for example, you buy a pair with a view to driving a four-wheeled vehicle, you may find that your existing arrangements for transporting animals and vehicles are suddenly inadequate for both!

If you are buying a 'made' pair, you should ask for at least one demonstration drive before purchase, to ensure compatibility. If you are not, then there is the question of obtaining a good match. This requires looking not only at factors such as height and length of stride, but also temperament, both in terms of whether the animals are equally free-going, and whether they like each other. On average, most animals are happier working as a pair once they know each other and get on well. If, however, they can't stand each other and keep trying to bite each other, even in harness, forget the whole idea until either they have sorted out their differences in the field at home, or the trouble-maker has been sold on and replaced with one who is more reasonable.

Regarding colour, although it is nice to have a match, a complete contrast such as a grey with a very dark bay can look attractive. In the early days, however, this matter is less important than matches in the other areas mentioned.

If you can surmount the question of cost, and find a well matched pair, driving them can be highly pleasurable and rewarding. Driving a pair of well balanced, well schooled animals to a comfortable vehicle with your family or friends on board is one of the most pleasant and exhilarating experiences you can have in driving. The satisfaction of a pair of animals working together as one, answering to their individual names, going in step, sharing the work evenly (uphill or down), makes the time and patience that has gone into training really worthwhile. The fact that more members of the family and/or friends can go out together is a great advantage. Obviously, this does depend on the type of vehicle used; a Body Break or Waggonette will carry more people than a four-wheeled Dog Cart or Ralli. A good, strong pair of 14.2 hh – 15.2 hh cobs, Gelderlanders or Hackney types can manage six humans on board reasonably easily. Obviously, they must not all be grossly overweight nor must the terrain be exceptionally hilly.

Pair Harness

Pair harness for driving a four-wheeler differs in several ways from single harness. Since they don't have to carry the weight of the shafts, the pads are narrower than a single pad. Rather than having a back band carrying tug loops, pair pads usually have short straps each side which buckle to the trace buckles and do no more than hold up the traces and the breast collar (if used). Instead of dart holes to go over the trace hooks, the traces have running loops with metal squares at the end to go over the roller bolts on the splinter bar, or some other form of loop. Vehicle braking, instead of being on the breeching fixed to the shafts, is by pole chains or straps fixed to the pole head. These are fixed to the harness by 'D's sewn onto the front of the breast collars, or, on full collars, to the rings sliding on the kidney links joining the bottom of the hames together. For safety these kidney links should be fixed to the collar either by separate short straps or by passing the martingale round the collar and kidney links. Alternatively, the pole straps can be passed round the throat of the collar.

The reins of pair harness which run from the bits to the hands are called draught reins. Shorter coupling reins are buckled to a series of holes about halfway along the draught reins.

When descending hills the animals, if wearing full collars, take the braking on the backs of their necks on the top of the collar. Since the pole straps run at an angle from the bottom of the collar to the pole head, the collar will tend to twist round the animal's neck. In seeking to avoid the discomfort this causes they will soon learn that, by leaning against the outside trace, they can keep the collar vertical. Therefore, they soon learn the disagreeable habit

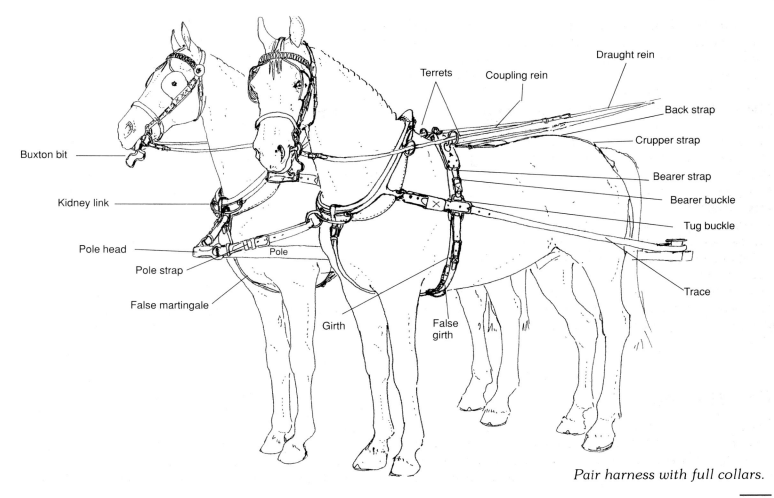

Buxton bit

Kidney link

Pole head

Pole strap

False martingale

Terrets

Coupling rein

Draught rein

Back strap

Crupper strap

Bearer strap

Bearer buckle

Tug buckle

Pole

Trace

Girth

False girth

Pair harness with full collars.

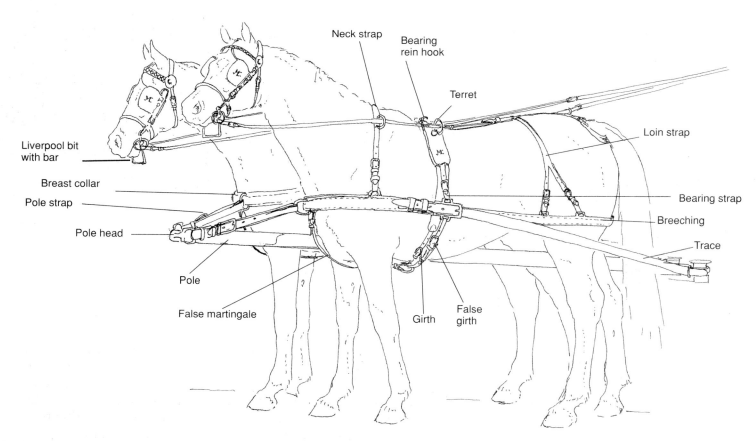

Neck strap

Bearing
rein hook

Terret

Loin strap

Liverpool bit
with bar

Bearing strap

Breast collar

Pole strap

Breeching

Pole head

Trace

Pole

False martingale

Girth

False
girth

Pair harness with breast collars.

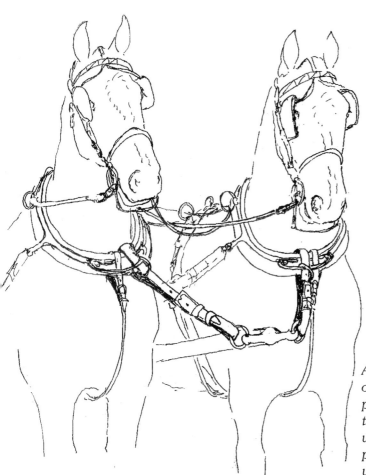

Alternative arrangements for pair harness. The practice (above) of using short pole straps fitted to a cross bar on the end of the pole (as used with agricultural machines) is uncommon in Britain, though popular in America. It prevents the collars being twisted when descending hills. The safety measure (left) of putting the pole straps round the collar as well as through the link is often used in cross-country driving.

of swinging their quarters out when going downhill. This can be prevented in two ways. First, in the American style, a cross bar can be used at the pole head, the same length as the distance apart of the animals. The pole straps are connected to the ends of this bar and so run straight forward in line with the animals. Secondly, breeching which transfers the braking from the animals' necks to their quarters can be used. The breeching consists of one long strap per animal, buckled to the trace buckles under the traces and going round the animals' quarters. It is held up by a loin strap which may carry a trace carrier loop under the breeching.

Harnessing Up

The harness is fitted in the same order as single harness; collar, pad, breeching and traces, reins and bridle. The pole straps are looped onto the pole head. Any buckles which may require adjusting after the animals are put to should be on the side of the animal further from the pole. This includes the noseband, top hame strap (the points of the two hame straps should face each other) and the girth buckle if there is only one. This also applies, if there is only one buckle, to the neck piece of the breast collar, the loin strap and the false belly band.

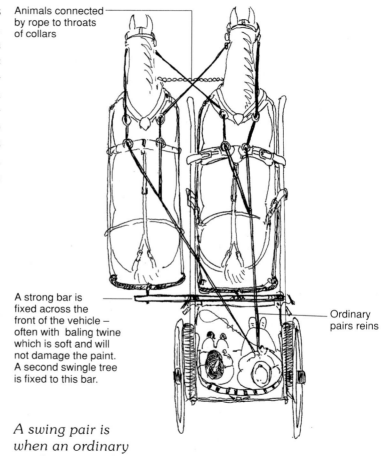

Animals connected by rope to throats of collars

A strong bar is fixed across the front of the vehicle – often with baling twine which is soft and will not damage the paint. A second swingle tree is fixed to this bar.

Ordinary pairs reins

A swing pair is when an ordinary single turnout has a second animal harnessed alongside.

Putting To

Once all is ready, the whip and clothing are either on the vehicle or being worn, and you are sure that you will not need to leave the animals, they can be put to the vehicle. To do so safely requires the help of an assistant.

One animal should be led into position alongside the pole with one hand, while the other hand guides him close to the pole by pressure on his side. Watch that the animal does not hit the splinter bar (or snag his harness) by walking sideways or backwards.

Once he is in place, he should be held by your assistant while you attach the pole chain or strap on its longest setting. This helps to keep the animal in place, but allows freedom to hook on the traces easily. The outside trace, the one further from the pole, should be hooked on to keep the animal's quarters in place, and followed by the inside trace. Should you have a kicker, put him to first and fasten the inside trace by reaching over the pole from the other side. Since the leather tabs on the end of the traces are to help with their release, it seems logical to fit them so that they are both on the side of the trace further from the pole and therefore at their most accessible. All four traces should be set to the same length because any difference in the length of the animals is less noticeable if their shoulders are level.

The second animal should be led into place and put to in the same way. The pole chains or straps should then be tightened to their working position. They should be loose enough so that they do not become tight at the same time as the traces. On the other hand, they should not be so loose as to allow the splinter bar or the front wheels to hit the animals when going downhill. Tight pole straps will encourage the animals to lean away from the pole and pull against each other whereas, if they are too loose, you will be lengthening and shortening the reins excessively as you go up and down hills.

Finally, the coupling reins should be buckled to the bits, that of the animal with the higher head carriage crossing on the top of the other so that the movement of each animal's head does not affect the other. Initially, the coupling reins should be 7–10 cm (3–4 in) longer than the draught reins. Final adjustment can only be made after initially driving the animals.

With experienced animals and a good assistant, time can be saved by putting both to simultaneously.

Taking Out

Taking out is done in the reverse order from putting to, but great care must be taken when leading the animals forward and away from the pole. If a rein or piece of harness should catch on the pole head a nasty accident could follow. Again, two people are required.

Driving Pairs

In many ways, driving a pair is the same as driving a single. The rein handling is the same and so are the words of command. The differences arise from persuading the animals to work together. They should move off together and at the same speed; they should share the draught equally; they should change gait together and should hold back equally when descending hills. Achieving this ideal depends almost entirely on the coachman. If you think of two people lifting the same end of a heavy object, neither can tell whether they are taking their fair share of the weight. This is because neither knows the total weight of the object. The same applies to a pair of driving animals, with the additional problem that the 'weight' is constantly changing with the hills. It is therefore the Whip's job to ensure that each does his fair share of the work.

The second concern for the coachman is to ensure that the animals respond together to his commands. This is particularly important when moving off. Having, as with the single, made the animals stand still for at least five seconds after being released by the groom, the Whip orders 'Walk on'. It is very unlikely that both will respond at the same moment. The less responsive animal will need encouragement a moment before the 'Walk On', either by calling his name, or by touching him with the whip. If this is not done, the keener animal may well start forward into his collar, only to be met by the resistance of the other against the breeching. The keen animal will then stop just as the other starts and the same problem is repeated, only the other way round. This, at best, results in a rough start and, at worst, in a broken trace or rearing animal. The same applies to the change of gait to trot.

Once the animals are moving, you can begin to check the setting of the coupling reins. If one animal's traces are slack and he is up to his bit, then the coupling reins need adjusting to allow him to move further forward. If he is not up to his bit, then he needs encouraging with the whip. To let an animal move further forward, his coupling rein must be lengthened by moving its buckle forward on the draught rein over his partner's back. This, however, will also have the effect of moving his head away from the pole. Therefore, his own draught rein must also be moved forward, but to avoid this affecting the other animal, the other draught rein must be shortened by the same amount. The rule is therefore, that to move one animal into or out of draught, the coupling buckles should be moved by the same amount but in opposite directions.

Once the animals are working reasonably well together, you can see whether the coupling reins need adjusting to set them the right distance away from each other. They should be as close together as possible without bumping against each other or the pole. At the same time, their heads should be in line with their bodies. To turn their

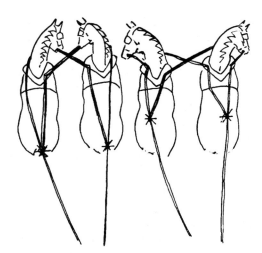

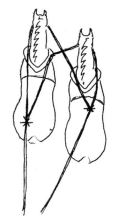

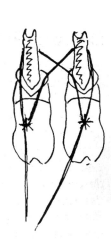

To turn the animals' heads towards each other, move both coupling buckles back the same amount. To turn their heads apart, move both buckles forwards

To let offside animal go forward into draught, move near coupling buckle forward and off coupling buckle back the same amount

To let near horse go forward into draught, move off coupling buckle forward and near coupling buckle back the same amount

The principles of adjusting the coupling reins. Note: after initial adjustment, further setting may be needed to match the angle of the animals' heads.

101

heads apart, both coupling reins should be lengthened and to turn their heads together, both should be shortened. The rule therefore is that to move the animals together or apart, the coupling buckles should be moved by the same amount and in the same direction.

Dealing with Problems

When descending hills, the less willing animal of the pair may well hold back too much and start slipping and, unless corrected, may even come down. In this case, although it seems unnatural on a slippery hill, you may have to push this animal on with the whip.

It can, in fact, be difficult to encourage a lazy animal without making the other pull even more. If you rely on general word command, the willing animal will respond more than the lazy one. The same applies to the use of the whip, unless it can be done quietly. The best answer is, if possible, to train each animal to respond to his own name. If one animal is extra keen, setting the bits differently for each can help; a lower rein setting and perhaps a tighter curb chain being used on the keener animal.

Pairs have a nasty habit of leaning onto, or away from, the pole. Fortunately, leaning consistently to the right or left is less common. Leaning away from the pole can, as previously mentioned, be caused by short pole straps – especially on a short pole – and by lack of breeching. Both

problems can usually be cured by moving the animals to the other side of the pole. During training, this may have to be done several times during a drive. A piece of hedgehog skin tied to the pole may also be effective when they are leaning towards each other. Remember, it takes two to pull and if you can stop one pulling away from the pole, the other may stop automatically. This can sometimes be done by driving the offender on the nearside, close to the edge of the road, when the verge or curb may stop him pulling out. If all else fails, a return to single driving for a short time may be effective.

Notwithstanding the above, the more novice or traffic-shy animal should be used on the nearside when possible, where he will be less likely to cause danger by swinging out into the traffic.

Pairs have a natural desire to work in step, but will usually only do so in practice if they have the same length of stride. This can be encouraged by making the shorter-striding extend. Ideally, at trot, they should be exactly 'out of step', that is to say, their footfalls should be simultaneous, but they should be on opposite diagonals to each other.

When slowing from trot to walk, it is easier to get a simultaneous change of gait if the speed is reduced to a very slow trot first, otherwise the animal with the faster walk will change first. This is also very good practise for driving in heavy traffic, when the ability to trot slowly allows you to fit in with the changing traffic speed.

Examples of Pair Vehicles

The Curricle and Cape Curricle are examples of vehicles specially designed to be driven to a pair.

The Curricle

The Curricle was a highly fashionable carriage driven with great dash by many of the early nineteenth-century characters who used it for travelling as well as town and park driving. Although it is a two-wheeled carriage it was built especially for a pair of horses to be driven one each side of the pole, which was suspended from a bar carried on the horses' backs. With the 'Tiger' (small groom) seated on the rumble seat, the carriage was perfectly balanced and was light and easy on the horses.

Harness for the Curricle. This differs from the usual pair harness in the pads. These are broad and well cushioned to distribute the weight of the Curricle and heavy pole at rest or in its unbalanced state. They also accommodate the built-in centre-roller terret which carries the bar. This special terret has a pair of rollers which can be adjusted in height so that the bar runs freely sideways to absorb the horses' slight sideways movements. The bar is prevented from sliding out of the terrets by disc nuts and split pins.

The girth is broad to take any pull from the balance strap which is threaded through its big loop keepers.

Putting To. This is not the carriage for an 'iffy' pair. Only well matched, steady horses should be put together in this way. Before putting to, the carriage must be prepared with the brace strap ready through the spring loop, the bar lying on the carriage and pole chains put on in the correct way. Pole chains rather than pole straps are used because this sporting turnout is owner-driven.

The Curricle carries its own folding stand which holds it firmly (at a height that will be the point of balance) while the horses are put to. Three people are needed for this procedure. The horses are brought from behind the carriage up either side of the pole. The reins are coupled, pole chains done up and traces placed on the swingle tree trace hooks (outside trace first). The bar is then held across the horses' shoulders and first one end then the other slid through the centre terret, the disc nuts screwed up and the flat safety split pin pushed home. Reaching in between the horses from the front, the broad carrying strap or brace is threaded through the slot in the centre of the bar and done up tightly, still leaving the carriage weight on the stand.

Next, the balance strap is brought from under the horses' bellies, passed through the large loop keepers and buckled on to the long 'point end' of the false girths and done up beside the false girth. With the pole chains adjusted, the horses are eased forward one stride, bringing

Curricle.

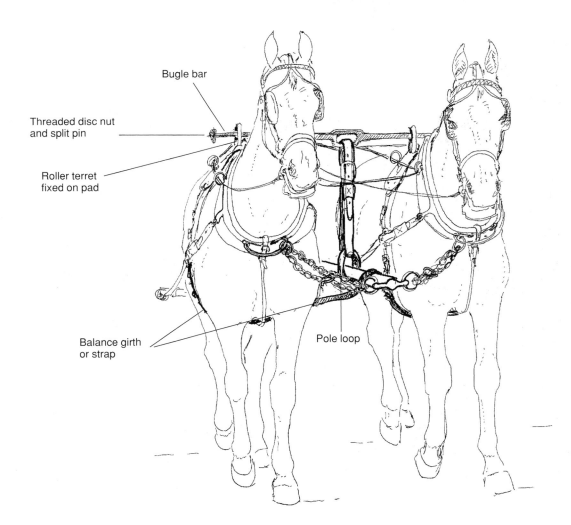

Bugle bar

Threaded disc nut
and split pin

Roller terret
fixed on pad

Balance girth
or strap

Pole loop

Curricle harness.

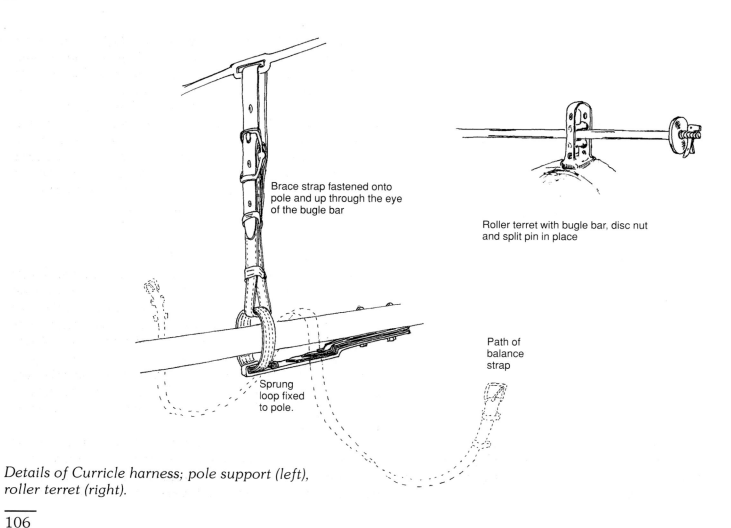

Brace strap fastened onto pole and up through the eye of the bugle bar

Roller terret with bugle bar, disc nut and split pin in place

Sprung loop fixed to pole.

Path of balance strap

Details of Curricle harness; pole support (left), roller terret (right).

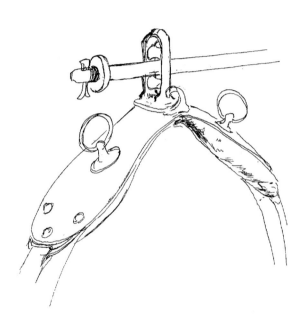

The broad Curricle pad distributes weight over a larger area of the animal's back than an ordinary pair pad. The latter is narrow because it has no weight to carry other than the traces.

the carriage off its stand so that the weight is taken on the horses' backs. With the groom still holding the horses' heads, one assistant reaches under from behind the horses and folds the stand back and holds it up under the carriage, while the second assistant secures it with its straps.

Alternatively, the stand may be secured up before the horses are put to, but a strong and patient assistant must hold the carriage up all the while. With the groom holding the horses' heads and one person doing up the brace strap this procedure creates rather a crowd at the pole head.

The procedure is reversed to take out.

Cape Harness or Cape Curricle

During the Boer War, the Cape Cart and the particular way of harnessing this light, two-wheeled vehicle to a pair was much admired by the English. This carriage enabled the Boer Generals to be where they were needed many miles away in amazingly quick time. After the war, Cape Carts were brought back to Britain and their method of carrying a centre pole for a two-wheeled carriage was adopted, being regarded as safer than the Curricle bugle bar fixed to the horses' backs. If one horse fell it was less likely to bring down the other.

The rather longer pole is suspended by a strap passing underneath it. This strap is then slung onto a strong, light-weight wooden bar which is carried by the harness from a yoke strap passing over the horses' necks beside the neck

Cape (or Cape Curricle) harness.

strap of the breast collar. This *draghout* or bar was used with ordinary, light breast collar harness.

There is a lot of movement of the pole, particularly when going at speed, and a balance strap can help to give a safer feeling as it prevents the pole from rising right up. Careful adjustment is needed both for this optional strap and the overall balance of the vehicle.

To Put To with Cape Harness. The horses are lead up each side of the pole and the coupling reins attached. The bar and pole are raised and held up while they are fixed and the pole straps done up. The traces are then put to the swingle trees. If a balance strap is to be used it is laid over the pole, reached for under the belly of the horses and passed through the martingale or loop keeper on the girth before going through the false girth. The order is reversed when taking out.

When using donkeys, it has proved better to place the bar under the pole as it interferes less with the donkeys, who have a naturally lower head carriage as well as longer heads in proportion to their depth of shoulder.

Although, with this vehicle, pad and breeching can be dispensed with, they do assist with keeping down the movement and chaffing of the collars.

If a pair of leaders is added to make a team, it will be necessary to add a hook to the pole end, from which to suspend the ordinary but light set of bars.

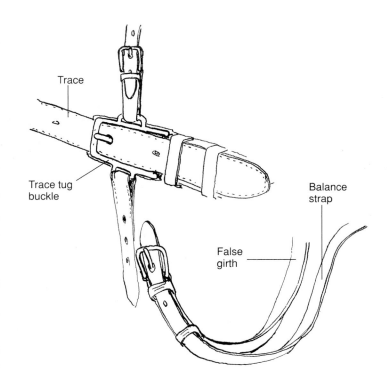

The balance strap passes through the keepers and buckle of the false girth, and then the false girth is done up in the usual way.

CHAPTER 12

Driving Tandem

Whereas, in a pair, the two animals are side by side, in tandem driving, they are one behind the other.

Tandem driving has always had a comparatively small following, but those who do drive a tandem are usually very enthusiastic. This is, perhaps, understandable since considerable skill and concentration are required and many people give up tandem driving after a short experience.

There is a certain increased risk in driving a tandem but, if we wanted to avoid difficulties and risk altogether,

we would only travel by car. Hopefully, the explanation which follows will convince you that a tandem provides an even greater measure of pleasure and interest than any other method of driving.

The fundamental difference in driving with four reins instead of two is that we are not provided with enough hands and fingers to be able to control four reins independently. You therefore have to guess how your animals will respond when turning, and 'take a loop' of appropriate size. Making this estimate of their response is dependent upon understanding both the animals and the situation and is one of the delights of driving a tandem, since it involves a mental communication, especially with your leader, and an increased awareness of your surroundings.

Driving a tandem is also the cheapest and, for most people, the most available method of practising handling four reins. The method is, in fact, exactly the same as driving a team, but has the advantage of requiring less strength. The rein handling needs to be quicker and more sensitive than in team driving and it is therefore an excellent preparation for four horses which is, probably, the ultimate goal for most Whips.

Making a start in tandem driving is not expensive, but obviously requires, as an absolute minimum, two animals (who do not need to match in colour, type or size), two sets of single harness, any two-wheeled vehicle (though a Governess Cart is the least suitable) and six lengths of baling twine. The twine is used to connect the leader's traces to the wheeler's trace buckles and to extend the leader's reins at the front end. You will also need two small loops of string on the ends of the wheelers' browband to carry the leader's reins. This would be sufficient (taking care that the makeshift reins do not jam), to give you an introduction to handling four reins.

Such simple beginnings could lead eventually to membership of a most interesting and exclusive group of people, the Tandem Club. The original Tandem Club was started in the 1860s by army officers, who used two of their hunters in tandem to provide themselves with excitement. The club was rather short-lived, but was revived in 1977 by Sallie Walrond and Lady Cromwell. To this day, the club maintains the original aim that 'there should be no joining fee, and the annual subscription should not, on any account, exceed the joining fee'! The only qualification required is the ability to drive a tandem safely and well.

In FEI competitions, while the single horse and pony classes are oversubscribed, the tandem classes are comparatively small and elite.

Today, the *practical* advantages of tandem driving are very few, although there have been situations in the past where the strength of more than one animal was required but a pair was impractical along narrow tracks or heavily wooded country. Nonetheless, tandem driving has always been, and remains, a glorious way of getting to know your animals and having fun and, perhaps, a little excitement.

A sporting tandem. The leader is ready to be ridden when the driving reins and breast collar are removed. The stirrups, connected under the belly, act as a trace carrier. With light webbing traces, a dark elastic can be used as a second trace carrier.

Tandem Vehicles

Any vehicle can be driven tandem, though a two-wheeled vehicle is safer and, under most conditions, preferable. This is because of the danger of the leader coming out of draught and the reins becoming slack; indeed there is the further danger of the leader turning to face you!. The safest action to take, should this occur, is to rein back the wheeler until either the leader's reins become tight, so regaining contact and control, or until the leader's traces come tight and pull the leader straight again. This procedure is explained more fully in the section on tandem driving. If this reining back is attempted with a four-wheeler, it is likely that the vehicle will jack-knife, so preventing the regaining of control. Also, as a four-wheeler jack-knifes, you will no longer be facing the animals, so making control even more difficult.

With two-wheeled vehicles, it is a great advantage to have a high seating position which gives a better view of the leader and a better position for using the whip, which is much more likely to be needed for the leader than the wheeler. The traditional high vehicles for tandems are Tandem Carts and Cocking Carts, so called because the height of the seats can give a backward and forward motion to the occupants, rather like a rooster walking. Both vehicles are difficult to balance because of their height and are therefore provided with bodies mounted on steel rods. The body can be slid along these rods by a handle to correct the change of balance when passengers mount or dismount.

The one occasion when a four-wheeled vehicle may be preferable is FEI competition driving. In this discipline there is, at present, some enthusiasm for four-wheelers, which give a more comfortable ride and a firmer base for control than a two-wheeler. Careful training and planning are relied upon to overcome the inherent disadvantages. It is, however, important that the vehicle should have a full lock which allows the front wheels to turn at least to right angles to the centreline of the vehicle. There still remains the inherent instability of a four-wheeler which, when on full lock, becomes in effect a three-wheeler. The higher the proportion of weight carried by the front wheels, the more likely the vehicle is to overturn.

Tandem Harness

The harness used for the wheeler or shaft horse is an ordinary single set of full collar harness with a few added features.

On the bridle there are roger rings welded to the rosettes or, sometimes, drop terrets carried on the throatlash. The bridle must fit particularly well, so that there is no danger of the extra weight of the leader reins pulling it off. Lead reins running through a drop or flying terret cause

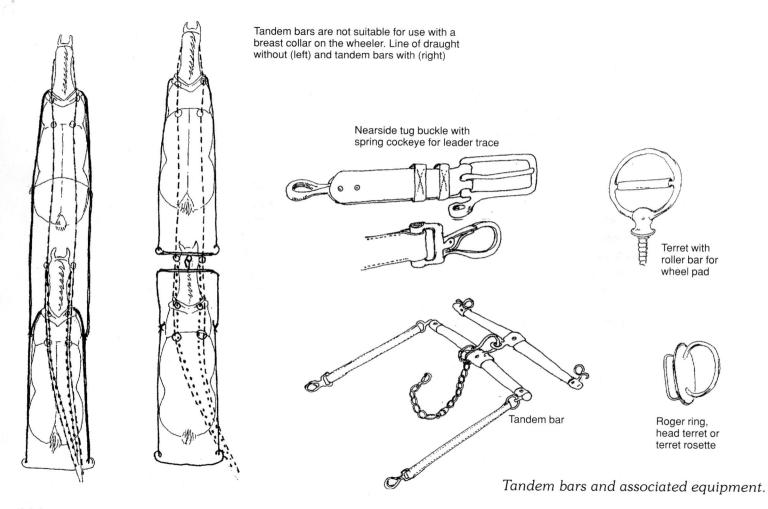

Tandem bars are not suitable for use with a
breast collar on the wheeler. Line of draught
without (left) and tandem bars with (right)

Nearside tug buckle with
spring cockeye for leader trace

Terret with
roller bar for
wheel pad

Tandem bar

Roger ring,
head terret or
terret rosette

Tandem bars and associated equipment.

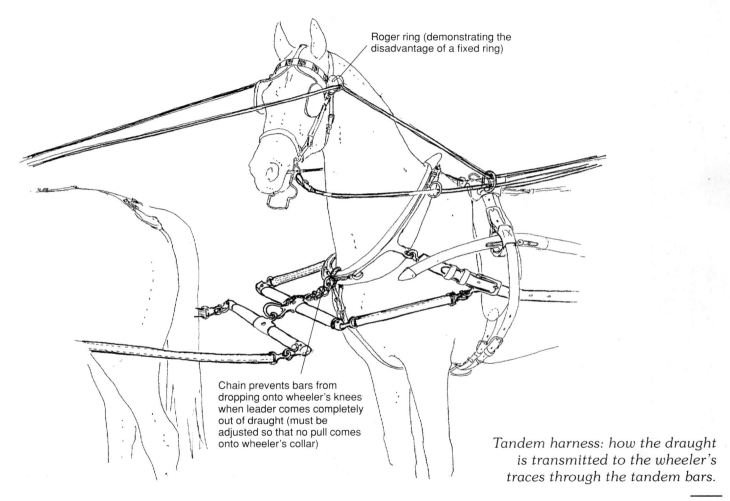

Roger ring (demonstrating the disadvantage of a fixed ring)

Chain prevents bars from dropping onto wheeler's knees when leader comes completely out of draught (must be adjusted so that no pull comes onto wheeler's collar)

Tandem harness: how the draught is transmitted to the wheeler's traces through the tandem bars.

*A tandem turnout showing the
line of draught through the traces and the
direct link of the reins via a flying or drop terret.
A breast collar could be used on the leader.*

less interference with the wheeler than the more traditional roger ring.

Terrets on the pad are often divided horizontally with a roller bar, so that the reins run separately and smoothly within the same ring.

The hames sometimes have their terrets divided in the same way, even though they are not often used for the lead rein. The two hames are either joined at the throat of the collar by a chain which has a centre ring, or joined with a kidney link with a free-running ring on it. The purpose of this ring is to carry the chain from the tandem bars, if used. The hame tug buckle has a protrusion on its lower edge which has a rounded, vertical hole through it. This is to receive either the snap cockeye of the leader trace or the tandem bar trace.

The tandem leader's harness is light and consists of a bridle and long reins of the appropriate length. There is a light pad with keepers sewn lying flat for the traces to pass through. Alternatively, a leader pair pad can be used with a breast collar or collar and hames. The back strap is sometimes of the martingale pattern, usually with a crupper dock sewn on. The advantage of this is that the tongue of the buckle lies toward the animal's tail, presenting a smooth surface with no hazard for the reins to catch on. The disadvantage is that there may be no place provided to take the loin strap of the trace carriers.

Ordinary single breast collar or collar and hames are used. The traces finish in a snap cockeye and are either long enough to go back on to the wheeler's hame tug buckle, or of the appropriate length to be used with the tandem bars. Sometimes, there is a light strap and buckle or 'D' set in the lower edge of the trace to connect the two traces under the belly of the animal, so preventing them from rising up over the leader's back (which can happen in extreme or tricky situations). Provision to keep this strap from swinging back may be provided on the girth in the form of a keeper.

Harnessing in Tandem

The Wheeler is harnessed in the ordinary way as for single driving. The reins are put up through the back strap using the usual quick-release method. If tandem bars are used they are put on after the wheeler is put to.

The Leader is also harnessed in the usual way, with the traces being put safely up. Short traces are wound in a knot or put over the back under the back strap. If trace carriers are being used, the ends are folded over the trace in front of the carrier. With the long traces it is usual to snap the cockeyes onto the terrets of the pad.

The reins are put on separately either side of the animal in preparation for putting to (the rein with the joining buckle being on the offside). The buckle and billet ends are passed through the pad and collar terrets ready to buckle to the bit. The long rein is then drawn back and folded

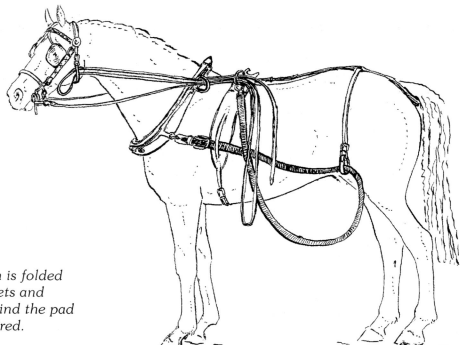

Harnessing the tandem leader. The lead rein is folded double and passed forward through the terrets and throatlash, with the hand piece hanging behind the pad so that it will run smoothly back when required.

double and the loop passed back through the terrets, leaving the hand piece hanging behind the pad.

Putting To

The tandem' wheeler is put to as for single driving. The leader is then brought quietly beside and past the wheeler and stood in place – this is safer than backing him in or bringing him in facing the wheeler and then pivoting him round.

With long traces. The reins are drawn back free from the terrets with a steady pull on the hand piece and threaded through the roger ring and top section of the pad terret.

When both are through, all four reins are put up on the wheeler's pad or back strap ready for the Whip.

The groom standing at the head of the wheeler can now control both animals. Having checked that they are not twisted, the lead traces are taken down and snapped into place on the wheeler's trace buckles. The animals are now ready to be driven.

With tandem bars and shorter traces. When the wheeler is put to, the bars are held up in place while the support chain is threaded upwards through the ring in the centre of the wheeler's hames. The snap hook is then closed on one of the links so that the opening is facing downward. The cockeyes of the bar traces are then snapped into the trace buckle eyelets. Next, the length of the chain is adjusted so that when the leader comes into draught no pull will be transmitted to the collar. The leader is then led into place and the reins put up as previously described and the traces are hooked onto the lead bars.

Tandem Driving Techniques

There are several different techniques for handling four reins, but the two basic systems are the English, which is more suitable for road driving, and the Hungarian (or FEI) method for competition driving. The relative advantages are that the English style allows for full use of the whip and shortening the reins when descending hills and the FEI style allows faster and more accurate control of the animals in tight situations.

In the English style of driving, all the reins are held in the left hand at a setting which keeps the animals going straight forward. The right hand controls the steering, lengthening and shortening the reins in the left hand, and uses the whip and the brake. The reins may be held in the left hand in one of two methods: the traditional and the 'full hand'. The traditional left hand position is with the nearside lead rein over the index finger and the offside lead rein under the index finger. The nearside wheel rein is held over the second or longest finger against the offside lead rein which is already there, and the offside wheel rein is held over the third finger. You will see that all the reins can now be led down through the hand and locked in position by the two lower fingers. The only disadvantage of this style is that the two middle reins are likely to slip, since each of them is only held against your glove on one side. In the 'full hand' style, the lower two reins are moved down one finger, but the disadvantage here is that the lower rein, the offside wheel, is only held by the little finger and is likely to slip. The traditional style is the more often used.

The right hand can be used in several ways, but in all styles the principle is the same. When turning a corner, the leader and wheeler need to be set at an angle to each other, or articulated. If this is not done and the animals are driven in the American 'Wells Fargo' style, with all the left reins in the left hand and all the right reins in the right hand, then the wheeler will cut the corner and turn inside the track of the leader. In the wide open spaces of the American West this didn't matter and, in fact, their vehicles usually had large front wheels which rode better over rough ground but would not lock under the body for sharp turns. In England, though, the problem was different; it was necessary to turn corners keeping the animals on their own side of the road and the vehicle off the pavement. The English therefore developed the system of articulation, which allowed a coach driver to turn the leader (or leaders, of a team) at right angles through the narrow arch of a coaching inn, followed accurately by the wheeler(s) and the coach. You will notice that most English vehicles also have small front wheels, allowing a sharp lock.

The methods by which articulation can be achieved vary and, in the interests of a complete description of driving techniques, let us look at each separately:

The English Method

This consists of taking a guess at the amount of rein that needs to be shortened to take the leader round a corner. This is then taken up by the right hand into a loop under the left thumb. This then leaves the right hand, which is also carrying the whip, to steer the wheeler and therefore the vehicle round the corner. The system operates as follows:

To turn to the left, take a loop of the nearside lead rein – the top one – with the right hand and place the loop under the left thumb. This will start the leader turning to the left. To prevent the wheeler from following, the offside wheel rein should be picked up by the right hand, so putting 'opposition' onto the wheeler. The amount of opposition can be varied whilst rounding the corner to keep the wheeler following in the tracks of the leader. When the leader has rounded the corner, the loop can be slipped smoothly to bring the leader straight, and the wheeler's reins can be allowed to return to the straight ahead position a few moments later, when the wheeler has also rounded the corner.

To turn to the right, a loop is taken in the offside lead rein and held under the left thumb. Opposition is held on the nearside wheel rein in the same way as for turning left.

When driving straight, the 'three rein trick' will be found helpful. For this, the right hand holds the two nearside reins with the lead rein between the first and second fingers and the wheel rein between the second and third fingers. The heel of the right hand rests on top of the two offside reins, which are then used together, so reducing the number of reins in effect to three. To bring the leader to the left, grip the nearside lead rein and bring the right hand back, allowing the other reins to slip. To bring the wheeler to the left, use the same system on the nearside wheel rein. To bring both animals to the left, grip both the nearside reins and take them both to the right, bear down on the two offside reins with the edge of the right hand, while releasing the nearside reins. This gives full control for gentle turns but does not, of course, give any articulation. To shorten or lengthen the reins, put the right hand against the front of the left hand, with the reins passing between the fingers in the same way as in the left hand. The right hand can then hold the reins without them slipping while the left hand is slid backwards or forwards. For an emergency stop, the right hand is held in the same position on the reins, slid forward to grip them firmly and used for a quick stop. This method does not permit steering whilst stopping but, in an emergency, the stop is so rapid that this is not usually important.

The Hungarian or FEI Method

Historically, the Hungarians had to cope with unsurfaced tracks which turned to glutinous mud during the winter. Their solution was to use high-mettled stallions, often in teams of five, to tow light, four-wheeled vehicles. Such horses are difficult to hold and control from a low seating position, so a system of driving was evolved with the reins buckled to a handpiece called the 'frog', which is rather like holding a suitcase handle in each hand. This eliminated the risk of reins slipping in the hand and gave great power over the horses. The problems were that the reins could not be lengthened or shortened quickly, nor could the leaders be taken readily into or out of draught.

Nevertheless, this system of driving has now been adapted for use in the cross-country and cone phases of FEI competition and provides quicker and more accurate control than the English method. The reins are buckled together rather than to a handpiece; the nearside lead to the nearside wheel and the offside lead to the offside wheel. The advantage of dispensing with the hand piece is that the reins can now be fed through the hand to vary the draught between the leader and the wheeler. The lead reins enter the hand from the top over the index finger and the wheel reins pass under the little finger. The nearside reins are held in the left hand and the offside reins in the right hand.

Since both hands are holding reins, it is not possible to use the whip without interfering with the animals' mouths, so a suitable moment has to be chosen for using the whip.

Articulation is still possible with this style of driving by taking loops on the lead reins and holding them under the thumb. This is done with the opposite hand and so quickly in the heat of competition that the momentary interference with the steering is too brief to cause a problem. With a tandem, the animals are so much more responsive than a team, so a useful amount of articulation can be achieved by twisting your wrist. With the back of the hand in the correct position (facing the horses), twisting your hand back, knuckles to the sky, towards your body, will tighten the lead rein and slacken the wheel rein. If this action is carried out with both hands, but in opposite directions, the animals will be articulated ready for a corner and, by moving one hand forward and the other back, the corner can be taken. To turn left, the left hand should be rotated back and vice versa to turn right. Driving a free-moving tandem fast through a slalom of cones by this method is one of the most satisfying experiences in driving.

What Can Go Wrong

It used to be said that a tandem driver should carry a loaded revolver to shoot the leader between the eyes should he turn to face him. Fortunately, this is no longer considered necessary. This situation is, however, probably the most difficult to correct for two reasons. First, since the leader is coming towards you, his reins will, of course, become loose and contact and control will be lost and second, if he gets so far alongside the vehicle that his reins do come tight, he will get such a jab in the mouth that he may rear or fall over.

The solution, as always in driving, lies in good training and prompt, unhurried correction without panic. The first action is to say 'Whoa', which should bring everything to a standstill while you sort out the tangle. If you have, as you should, an active groom, ask them to escort the leader back into place; if you do not, a tap with the whip on the leader's nose, which will be conveniently alongside you, may encourage him to re-position himself. Tandem leaders are very used to feeling where they are in relation to the turnout by the pressure of the traces, so it is safer to pull the leader straight with the traces by backing the wheeler, rather than by pulling the reins. This is the time when you will be pleased to be driving a two-wheeler rather than a four-wheeler!

Notwithstanding the above, a useful party trick to cultivate when standing about with a tandem with nothing much to do, is to fold the leader back alongside the wheeler until you can touch his nose and then put him straight again with the reins. This will not only earn you the applause of your friends, but will ensure that you can always extricate yourself from this embarrassing situation. Practise, though, with a groom at the leader's head.

Having dealt with the most dramatic thing that can go wrong, let us consider the minor irritations.

The simplest to correct is a wheeler who does not follow behind the leader. In the English style of driving, just move the two middle reins backwards or forwards through the left hand. In the Hungarian style, slide the leader's reins forwards through one hand and backwards through the other.

The problem which confuses most people is when the leader is too fast for the wheeler, or vice versa. The solution, provided that the reins were correctly set in the first place, is very simple. Move the left hand back if driving English style and both hands back if driving Hungarian.

What happens is that the pulling animal gradually takes all the rein contact and leaves the other horse's reins slack, therefore tightening the reins will only affect the puller, and will put matters right. Nevertheless, some animals are not sufficiently forward-going to make a tandem leader and there is really no way to drive these satisfactorily. However much you slow the wheeler, the leader will not keep up to the bit, and there is no way to control a driving animal without contact on the bit.

The opposite problem sometimes occurs, with a leader who is only happy in draught. This can cause problems because the wheeler's breeching is pulled tight by the leader and the wheeler, thinking that he must be going downhill, sits into the breeching. The extra load convinces the leader that he must be going uphill and he redoubles his efforts. The resulting tug-of-war makes the turnout impossible to drive. The way of preventing this is to keep the leader out of draught except when going up hills, when his help will be appreciated by the wheeler. Another way of looking at it is that the wheeler's breeching should never be tight except when descending hills, when the leader, of course, must be out of draught.

The secret of tandem driving is to find two animals who go together well; the leader forward-going and bold but responsive and controllable, and the wheeler calm, strong and unflappable. Although it is unlikely that the ideal tandem has ever been put together, a little-known trick for balancing the two animals may help. Short lead traces will slow the wheeler and long ones will encourage him to go forward. There are limits as to how long lead traces can be before you have problems with an animal getting a leg over when turning, but it is surprising how much difference 15 cm (6 in) will make. Try some baling twine and see what happens!

Mention of a leg over the traces brings us to the topic of tandem bars. These are two bars hung from the wheeler's collar, the one nearer him connected to his trace buckles by short traces and cockeyes, while the front one is connected to the leader's traces. The advantages of these are that ordinary single traces can be used for the leader, and that the traces are kept up by the wheeler's collar so there is less chance of a leg going over them. Tandem bars were more popular in the past, but most people now use long leader traces attached directly to the wheeler's trace buckles by cockeyes. This is simpler, lighter and removes the risk of the wheeler's teeth being hit by the swinging bar.

CHAPTER 13

Driving a Team

If finances permit, this is the next logical step after driving pairs, which will increase skills and interest in driving. Whether they are ponies or horses, the challenge and pleasure of getting four different 'beings' happy to work together with you is immense. The reasons why four animals are needed to pull one carriage may vary. It may be

that they are so small in stature that their combined power is needed to get the Whip and family to a picnic spot. Although the finances involved with a team of Shetlands are comparatively smaller than those encountered by the owner of a team of 17 hh horses, the amount of pride and fun gained from them can be the same. Many people want to drive teams, but only a few manage to realise this ambition.

In the nineteenth century, the strength of four horses was needed to pull coaches large enough to be commercially viable, though the amateur coachmen of the day sometimes paid for the pleasure of driving them in all weathers and through the night. There may have been pony teams put together, probably for ladies to drive, although we have to wait until the early 1900s to hear of the celebrated Miss Brocklebank and her expertise at four-in-hand driving.

More recently, when pony teams were included in FEI cross-country competitions, more people had the incentive and opportunity to acquire the skill of driving a team of four.

Carriage Choice for Teams of Four

The choice of carriage depends upon the purpose for which it is required as well as the size of animals to be put to it.

For cross-country carriage driving, a specialist-built carriage is essential. Finding the right one to suit both pocket and animals is a matter of watching others drive the different makes in competition and visiting the manufacturers' trade stands at the larger events.

For pony owners, whose aims are rally and pleasure drives on lanes and green roads, a Waggonette is ideal. A pairs vehicle can be used by adding a hook to the pole head, and a set of bars. There used, in the past, to be half- and three-quarter size coaches built especially for teams of ponies, although the originals are now very rare and expensive. Happily, though, there are good modern coach builders, who are able to build whatever you require.

For teams of large horses, Phaetons, Waggonettes, Breaks of all kinds, Charabancs and various coaches are available. However, all items on this long list are expensive and the comprehensive advice needed by a prospective purchaser is beyond the scope of this book. Our advice is to listen to many people and go to shows, collections of carriages and sales before taking the plunge with your cheque book.

Harness for Teams

The type of harness is largely dictated by the vehicle, and the purpose to which it is put. In general, breast collars are used for cross-country. Pony teams can either use breast collars, or, for more formal and show wear, a full collar set. In this country, horses put to a traditional vehicle wear full collars. Styles of collar, and details of harness for Park Drags and private use differ from that used for commercial vehicles. Although nowadays accepted in the show ring as a vehicle owned by a private person, a Road Coach is classed as a commercial vehicle.

Harnessing a Team

To harness up a team of horses or ponies, follow the usual procedure as for pairs. When the leaders' reins are put on, the length of rein can be run forward through the terret, pad and collar and the loop pushed through the throatlash.

When putting to, the wheelers are lead from behind the coach up each side of the pole to the pole head and put to in the same way as for a pair. It is a matter of choice whether the bars are already on the pole head or are put on now. The leaders can stand in place a little forward while the wheelers are put to, or can be brought up into position from beside the wheelers (not backed into place) when required.

The coupling reins may be coupled before the leaders are brought in, or they can now be done up and the draught rein passed through the roger ring and centre terret on the wheeler pads.

The nearside rein is thrown over to the offside after a verbal warning to the groom working on that side. The reins are then put up onto a wheeler's back, or handed to the Coachman if he is already on the box seat.

Next, both the lead traces are attached to the bars – offside first, then nearside. The second leader is then attached in the same way. If a coupling strap is to be used between the leaders' collars, this is now fixed. This is an innovation of cross-country carriage driving competitions. Its use is not correct with traditional English harness, but it is acceptable on the grounds of safety. Taking a team out is done in the reverse order from putting to, except that all animals must be freed from the coach and each other before any is moved away.

Driving a Four-in-hand

Although the reins are held in the same way as for tandem driving, with the fingers and hand having similar effects, the movements will not be so small. In team driving, problems are different and the safest and most enjoyable way to learn is to sit up beside a good four-in-hand Whip and watch, taking a 'handful' for a short time in easy stages. The weight of four horses, light-mouthed though they may be, is quite a shock to arm and shoulder, even if you are fit from driving pairs or tandem.

Practise at home with a driving machine will help to accustom the hand and arm to both weight and fingering

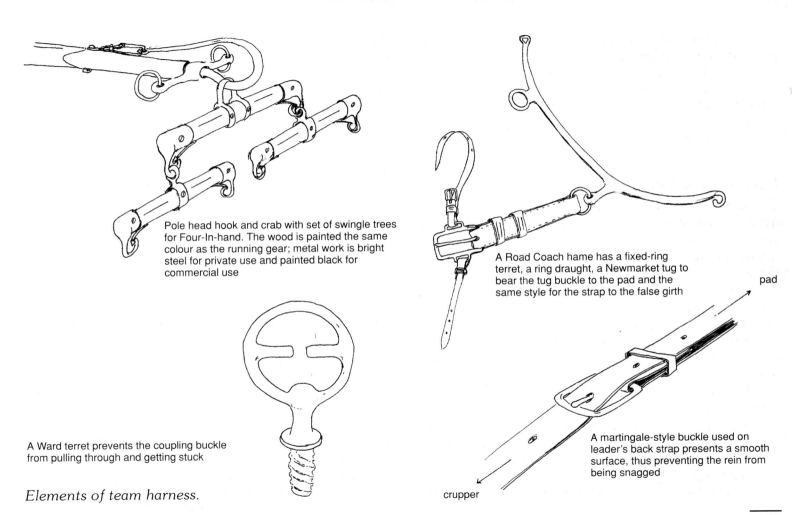

Pole head hook and crab with set of swingle trees for Four-In-hand. The wood is painted the same colour as the running gear; metal work is bright steel for private use and painted black for commercial use

A Road Coach hame has a fixed-ring terret, a ring draught, a Newmarket tug to bear the tug buckle to the pad and the same style for the strap to the false girth

pad

A Ward terret prevents the coupling buckle from pulling through and getting stuck

Elements of team harness.

A martingale-style buckle used on leader's back strap presents a smooth surface, thus preventing the rein from being snagged

crupper

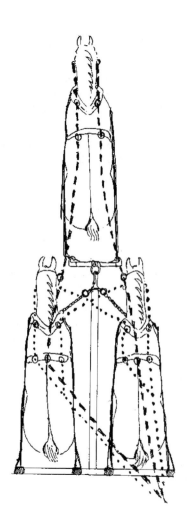

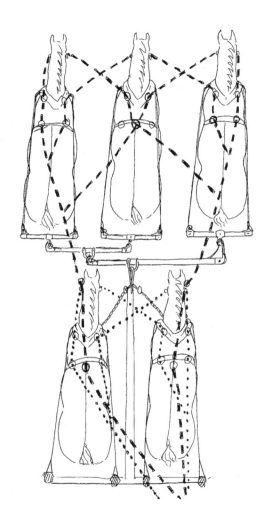

Arrangements of reins and traces for unusual teams; 'unicorn' (left) and 'pickaxe' (right).

and, if sitting high enough in a large enough space, you can practise using the whip. This not only entails learning the skill of being able to hit one leader where you want without upsetting the other animals but also retrieving the thong without snagging it in the trees or around the aerial of a passing car or, even worse, hitting your passengers and grooms who have so bravely come out with you! (Some Whips resort to a pocket of pea gravel and become very accurate at lobbing pebbles rather than unfolding the whip.)

Even when a degree of skill in manoeuvring the team has been achieved, the type of carriage will influence the way it is driven. For instance, if experience has been gained from the seat of a 'full lock' cross-country vehicle (with a low centre of gravity to cope with the gradients it has been designed for), it will come as some surprise to both team and Whip when encountering a quarter lock vehicle which weighs a lot more. Also, the height of the box seat and angle of reins may feel strange.

When moving off, it is extremely important that the wheelers and not the leaders actually start the coach. If this procedure is not followed, the wooden pole and bars of a traditional vehicle may snap, although the metal bars and sprung pole of a modern cross-country 'battle-waggon' will stand it. Plenty of practise in driving a restricted turning circle with only the wheelers moving the coach while the leaders just carry the bars is essential. The wheelers should be driven so that they do the work both up and down hill,

with the leaders just looking nice in front but ready to help instantly when needed, and moving along well out of the way when going downhill.

The fashion of using breeching with sporting coaches went out in the middle of the nineteenth century; with 'metalled' roads and iron-shod wheels, the wheelers probably wouldn't have been able to hold the heavy loads too well so, for lesser hills, trotting down with perhaps the use of an inefficient handbrake became normal (the Whip being ready to 'spring', or gallop the team up the next hill). For the longer and steeper hills, the coach halted on the brow in order to put on the skid pan or drag shoe, and a slow descent was made.

Nowadays, a cross-country team can keep on going fast, pulling against the disc brakes if required. The different difficulties met in the various types of driving today can only be learned safely under an experienced instructor.

Grooms, too, will encounter great variety. One day, dressed casually, throwing themselves in any way possible on and off a low back platform at speed; another, the vertical climb onto a coach in unison with each other, or the experience of the outward overhang of a Road Coach back seat. Woe betide them if they should scratch a panel in the process!

CHAPTER 14

The Show Ring

Before you attempt any show classes yourself, it is a good idea to go to various shows which have driving classes. As well as taking pleasure in spectating, you can observe the general procedure, and learn what is expected of the participants.

Spectating

In traditional coaching classes, the judge is looking at the animals' type and suitability for their coach and their conformation, as well as how nicely they go as a team. How they are bitted is a good indication of what the Whip may expect from them; if good manners and obedience are normal the reins will probably be set high. The judge is also looking to see that the whole turnout is presented nicely and is true to its traditions, which differ from type of coach to coach. The following are examples of traditional vehicles to which this applies.

The Park Drag

The Park Drag is relatively light in construction and painted in colours of the owner's choice; usually sombre. The monogram or badge of the owner is painted small on the doors and, perhaps, on the hind boot, which is hinged at the bottom and lets down to make a table. The boot is fitted with two big boxes lined with zinc to hold wine, ice and glasses, sometimes with a drawer above. Traditionally, picnic food was carried in one of the boxes or, sometimes, in the 'imperial', a box which is carried on the roof between the 'lazy-backs' – back rests which are hinged to lie flat. The inside of the coach is lined with cloth (usually Melton) matching the cushions outside. A fully fitted coach will have hat straps on the ceiling and a mirror on the inside of one of the wooden stable shutters, which will be positioned up for the show ring. Sometimes, a commode is concealed under one of the seats! The lamps, traditionally, are carried inside along with the spare waterproof knee rugs. Spare harness is carried in the front boot, for which access is from the inside through a trapdoor set in the back of the seat. The basket hanging on the nearside by the rear roof seat is designed to hold walking sticks and umbrellas. Spare bars are carried at the back of the groom's seat with the main bar on the top, while a folding ladder travels hung on brackets underneath this seat. Pole head, chains and bar fittings are all of bright metal. The skid pan and chain are carried beneath the coach and are painted black. Two grooms in matching livery complete the turnout.

The Road Coach

The Road Coach, being originally for commercial use, is strongly constructed and heavier and more robust than the Park Drag. It is brightly painted and traditionally had its destination and stopping points emblazoned on its panels.

Usually, the coach itself had a name, which was painted on the underside of the footboard, on the door panels and on the rear panel.

When showing, spares are carried in the rear boot, nicely displayed and consisting of everything that could possibly be needed, including footboard lamp, water bucket, spare shoes and shoeing tools and a complete set of harness (a spare soft collar being carried on the nearside lamp bracket). The lamps are carried in position ready for use. The footboard sometimes has a clock on it with a timeplate with arrival times of different stopping places. The spare folding whip is carried on a board hanging underneath the front seat. The lazy-backs of the coach are rigid and straps run laterally between them on the edge of the coach, forming a luggage rack. The rear seat is wide enough for four people. The long basket on the nearside is for umbrellas, sticks and coach horn. From the rail of the rear seat the spare bars hang, the main one at the top. The folding ladder travels on hooks set under the rear boot. The inside of the coach is lined with wood with upholstered cushions matching the ones outside, often of Bedford cord or heavy material. Hat straps are provided on the ceiling and leather pockets on the insides of the doors. There are stable shutters but the coach is shown with its cottage windows exposed (the glass is divided into four or six small panels within its wooden frame). The door hinges are to the front of the coach so that the door will swing shut on setting off if it has been left open. The toe

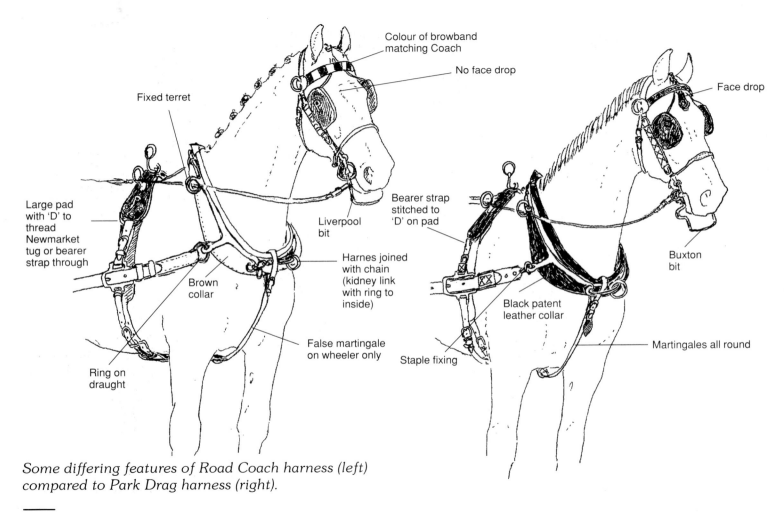

Fixed terret

Colour of browband
matching Coach

No face drop

Face drop

Large pad
with 'D' to
thread
Newmarket
tug or bearer
strap through

Brown
collar

Liverpool
bit

Bearer strap
stitched to
'D' on pad

Harnes joined
with chain
(kidney link
with ring to
inside)

Buxton
bit

Black patent
leather collar

Martingales all round

Ring on
draught

False martingale
on wheeler only

Staple fixing

*Some differing features of Road Coach harness (left)
compared to Park Drag harness (right).*

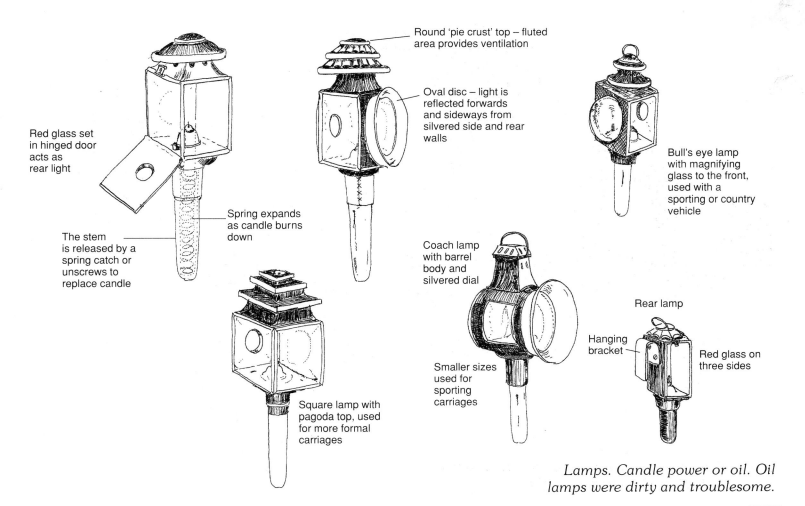

Red glass set in hinged door acts as rear light

The stem is released by a spring catch or unscrews to replace candle

Spring expands as candle burns down

Round 'pie crust' top – fluted area provides ventilation

Oval disc – light is reflected forwards and sideways from silvered side and rear walls

Bull's eye lamp with magnifying glass to the front, used with a sporting or country vehicle

Square lamp with pagoda top, used for more formal carriages

Coach lamp with barrel body and silvered dial

Smaller sizes used for sporting carriages

Rear lamp

Hanging bracket

Red glass on three sides

Lamps. Candle power or oil. Oil lamps were dirty and troublesome.

plates over the steps are of brass. The pole head chains and bar fittings are painted black, as is the skid pan and hook, which are carried underneath the nearside rear wheel.

The turnout is completed by the guard, who sits on the nearside of the rear seat. He wears a red frocked coat which has contrasting collars, cuffs and pocket flaps. Also, breeches worn with leggings and brown boots, a spotted cravat and brown gloves, with a felt beaver hat. Over his shoulder he carries a pouch, originally to hold the waybills, which often has a watch set in it and a key for the rear boot.

While horses for a Park Drag should match in colour, this is not so important for a Road Coach. If all four horses are of different colours they are called an 'odd' team. If there are two matching pairs they are usually set on opposite sides, leader from wheeler, in which case it is called a 'crossed' team. Very often, if there is one grey or odd-coloured horse, he is placed as the offside leader. This stems back to the days when, driving at night, the light-coloured horse showed up on the centre of the road.

Watching a Trade Class

There are many different types of vehicle shown in the light trade class. All should be working vehicles, painted and harnessed in an eye-catching way to advertise their wares. A flashy animal should also catch the eye but must,

at the same time, be well mannered. This may be demonstrated by the tradesman alighting, putting up his reins and leaving the animal to stand still for a minute. It will be noticed that mounting and dismounting are done from the

Trade harness. This has chain end traces and is enlivened with brightly coloured patent leather face drops, rib tappers and sweat pad.

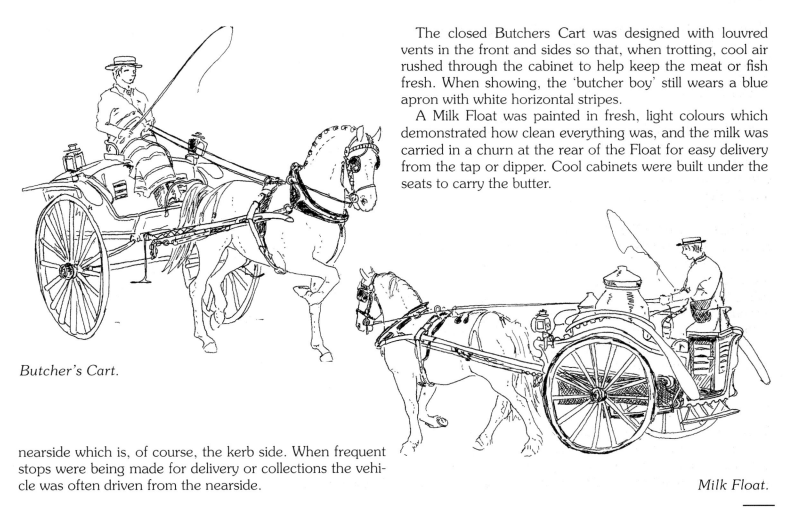

The closed Butchers Cart was designed with louvred vents in the front and sides so that, when trotting, cool air rushed through the cabinet to help keep the meat or fish fresh. When showing, the 'butcher boy' still wears a blue apron with white horizontal stripes.

A Milk Float was painted in fresh, light colours which demonstrated how clean everything was, and the milk was carried in a churn at the rear of the Float for easy delivery from the tap or dipper. Cool cabinets were built under the seats to carry the butter.

Butcher's Cart.

nearside which is, of course, the kerb side. When frequent stops were being made for delivery or collections the vehicle was often driven from the nearside.

Milk Float.

Flat-bed trolley with produce display.

Flatbed Carts or small Lorries used by fruiterers and greengrocers carried magnificent displays of fruit or vegetables, while the same type of vehicle was used by the rag-and-bone man to throw his scrap items on.

Smart Broughams or omnibus-style delivery vehicles are driven single or pair and painted in the traditional shop colours, with the shop name on the side. Liveried servants add refinement. Nowadays, shop goods are not carried in the show ring.

Some of the animals will be seen wearing rope halters under their bridles. This practice dates back to the Second World War, when parliament decreed that horses should wear halters beneath their bridles, so that they could be tied up in the event of an air raid.

Private Driving Classes

Technically, a private driving class is for animals of suitable temperament for a novice Whip to set up and drive without coming to any harm.

Sadly, however, there is a lot more emphasis these days on very free-moving, extravagant animals, such as Welsh Cob and Hackney stallions. While admirable of themselves, and spectacular in the hands of an experienced, confident Whip, many such animals would be by no means safe and easy for a novice to drive.

Since it is likely that your first experience of show ring driving will be in such a class, it is worthwhile paying extra attention to the criteria used for judging. Many of these criteria also apply to other classes, but this is an appropriate moment at which to examine them.

What the Show Judge Looks For

Judges all look for a turnout which is pleasing to the eye because it is balanced – that is to say, animal and vehicle are suitable for each other. They expect to see a well balanced, free-moving, obedient animal, well turned out in good quality, clean, correctly fitting harness, driven to a clean, safe, well maintained vehicle, with a correctly kitted-out spares box.

The turnout should be driven correctly, considerately and safely by a Whip who is dressed in an outfit which is neat and tidy but not flamboyant. The judge will assess the Whip's basic style, looking for a straight back, sloping thighs, reins held correctly and whip at the correct angle. He will also wish to see evidence of confidence; a slight smile gives a good impression, but a worried expression may make the judge think that something untoward is about to happen.

Good manners are also important, both from the animals and the Whips. A judge who is watching individual shows, or working down a line of inspection, will not take kindly to exhibitors who are slouched in their vehicles, chattering noisily or smoking.

A good driving position – wheel tops level with slightly sloping seat, reins in straight line between mouth and hand, rein rail preventing the reins from flapping.

Show Ring Technique

Style, elegance, composure and control are the first things that should spring to mind when watching a show class. How are these achieved? The choice of animal, harness and vehicle combined with training and feeding are the main ingredients. These must be blended with knowledge and skill in the art of horsemanship.

Newcomers to show ring driving are often completely puzzled as to why some turnouts do consistently well under many different judges, while others which may look perfectly correct to the beginner (but are, in fact, far from being so) are placed well down the line. It could be, for example (and this does happen quite often) that a non-sliding back band is being used to a single turnout, or maybe the animal being shown has a poor neck and would look better in a full collar. No matter how beautiful and expensive the harness, nor that the vehicle is an expensive, beautifully restored Lawton, if either of these faults appeared in competition with others who had well-used but clean, safe, correctly produced show harness or an ani-

Animal and vehicle compatible.

Animal and vehicle not well balanced.

mal with slightly poor conformation but correctly 'dressed' the latter examples would, in most cases, be placed higher up the line. In the first case, because of the safety factor and in the second, because the impression of balance would be preferable with the full collar disguising the ewe neck.

Horsemanship and expertise are two factors which go hand-in-glove and complement each other. Horsemanship comes with experience gained over years of working and schooling different animals. Every equine is different; in temperament, willingness, movement, speed, reactions, general manners and various other characteristics, which all teach the human who is interested a deeper understanding of horsemanship. Expertise comes from the experience of working with these animals. It is the consequential knowledge gained over a period of time and the use of that knowledge in developing the art of producing the best possible result on the day from a particular animal or animals.

Money alone cannot buy trophies. Sadly, there are people who think it can but, at the end of the day, it is usually the pure skill of horsemanship and production of a turnout

Illustrations to show the effect of driving a different animal to the same vehicle.

The judge's predicament.
Often seen in the show ring is a good type of cob put to an elegant vehicle. Though individually nice they are in no way matched. This type of turnout is often driven by a person idiosyncratically dressed, with a rein in each hand and the whip resting in the socket. Although animal and Whip may be thoroughly enjoying themselves, the overall picture is not conducive to first place!

that will win the class. Therefore, once the decision has been taken to commence show ring work, the vehicle and harness have been purchased and the animal has had experience of being in company, then show ring procedure and technique need to be considered and practised at home.

Procedure in the Collecting Ring

It is polite to reach the collecting ring at least ten minutes before the class is due to begin, to give the collecting ring steward time to check your number against the list of entries. More importantly, from your point of view, it also gives you a chance to settle your animal in his surroundings, by letting him walk around quietly. You may wish to have your groom on the ground near him; this will depend upon his general mood on the day. In addition to settling him, this period of gentle, calm warming-up stops him from becoming bored and gives you, the competitor, time to assess who else is forward for the class and where you would like to position yourself for entry into the ring.

Entering the Ring

If you have a free-moving animal it is usually advisable to go in ahead of a slower one. Alternatively if it is practicable to have quite a large space between turnouts in the ring and you have a free-moving animal, enter behind a slow one, leaving plenty of space. This is a very neat way of attracting the judge's eye, especially if you know that your animal carries himself well, and the one in front is slopping along.

Most judges like to see a class enter the ring at walk and keep walking until the ring steward asks them to trot on.

Show Ring Manners

It is usually considered bad manners to trot round the ring overtaking, especially on the inside. If the turnout in front is impeding your progress, take your animal further out into a corner and so open up a good space between you. If you have a free-moving animal who can extend well, you can let him extend as you pass in front of the judge, but do not break gait into canter – this is always considered bad manners. If there is an exhibitor who is constantly overtaking on the inside of the ring and appears to be doing so deliberately, the vast majority of judges, especially BDS panel judges, will notice this and invariably penalise them by dropping their placing in the line-up.

In an open class, with no height distinctions, if often seems that the smaller ponies do tend to take an inside line on their circling of the ring. If the class is not a very large one, the judge will often ask the ring steward to direct everyone back to the same track.

Changing the Rein

It is an important part of ringcraft to do this correctly. Take a positive diagonal line from where the steward gives his instruction and arm indication and drive to the far corner before turning to circle on the opposite rein. Remember to give whip signals to those following. It is usual to enter the ring on the left rein and drive round it initially on the right rein (clockwise) so, when the change of rein has been completed, you are back driving on the left rein (anti-clockwise). Again, keep your distance from the turnout in front, so that you can give a good show to the judge. If you know that your animal does not extend, keep a steady, safe distance (three or four lengths) from the vehicle in front of you as out on the road. After a few laps of the ring on the opposite rein, the judge will instruct the ring steward to bring everyone into line.

The First Line-up

At this stage there are two options open to the judge, who may either ask exhibitors to line up in any order, or have them lined up in order of preference at that stage. Either way is acceptable, but the steward should make it quite clear to exhibitors which is being done.

Once everyone has lined up, put your groom down to stand in front of the animal in the approved manner and, if you wish to use a loin rug, ask your groom to put it over the animal. Remember, do not have a rug with a sponsor's name all over it! Now the individual inspections take place. Usually the judge starts at the top of the line and works down, looking at the fit and cleanliness of the harness, balance and condition of the vehicles, and even making sure that the candles in the lamps have been lit. The spares box is also checked, especially if there is to be a show drive or marathon.

The Individual Display

If the class does not have a show drive then, at this stage, exhibitors are each asked to give an individual display. The judge will indicate, via the steward, exactly what type of display or show is required. However, the procedure is usually to walk out of line up to the end of the ring and then trot past the judge at a slight angle, so that, in effect, you can trot a figure-of-eight with some extension on the diagonal. On the last straight line come down to walk for four paces; halt in front of the judge; count four to yourself and rein back four paces; halt; count four; walk forward four paces; halt; count four and salute the judge. To salute, a lady bows her head and raises her whip horizontally in line with her forehead, while a gentleman raises his bowler. You then receive the judge's salute and move forward, preferably walking two or three paces then trotting, going to the far end of the line-up and round the back into line. Never go into line from the front.

If, during your display, your animal refuses to back after two or three attempts, move forward. Do not 'maul him in the mouth'; do your training at home. If the ground is sloping, always halt to rein back going down the hill; this is easier for the animal and always looks better.

In show classes with a road drive, the individual displays are often done on the return from the drive. In such cases the judge is looking for all the same things as in an ordinary show class but will also be looking to see how fit and calm each exhibitor's animal is; whether still collected and willing, or exhausted and in a white lather. While you were on the drive, the judge will have been watching to see how close you were to the vehicle in front (which should have been a minimum of three lengths, and preferably four, so that an overtaking car has room to pull in front of you). The judge will also have been watching to make sure your animal was not pulling your arms out and that you were driving and signalling in the correct manner.

After the individual displays, the judge will usually send the class out for a final lap or two before calling exhibitors into line in the final order. Sometimes, however, exhibitors numbers are called in reverse order. This can help in a small ring by giving the free-moving animals more scope to show themselves better.

The Final Line-up

The way you carry out your individual display can very

easily affect your position in the final line-up. No matter how expensive your harness or vehicle, no matter how costly your hat or clothes, if the harness does not fit correctly, if your animal is not obedient, if you have not exhibited good ring manners and given a good display, your final position in the line-up will disappoint you.

Remember, all of us and our animals can have off-days. This applies even to those who usually do everything correctly and are regular winners in the ring; they, too, have their off-days and must be prepared to go 'down the line'. This should always be done with good grace; it is the height of rudeness to argue with the judge. It is the judge's opinion on the day, combined with the amount of skill and technique you and your animal have been able to portray, that determines your final position.

After you have received your rosette, or not, as the case may be, once the signal has been given by the ring steward to move off, ask your groom to get back up into the vehicle and leave the ring in an orderly fashion.

Propriety

A point to remember during the class is, if you know the judge, do not speak to them by name. It should always be 'Sir' or 'Ma'am'. In the same vein, a judge should not speak to you using your name or instruct his steward to bring you in by name. A good judge (and most are) is not influenced by friendship on the day. In the ring they 'switch off' such relationships and judge what is in front of them on that day. Sadly, a great many exhibitors do not seem to understand this.

One final little hint. If you are nervous, your animal will be also. Equines can pick up from their handlers the nervous aroma that humans secrete. To avoid this, gentlemen Whips can put some aftershave on their hands and lady Whips can use perfume in the same manner. When harnessing up, make sure your animal sniffs your hand; this will help to prevent him from becoming jumpy. Remember, singing does not cover the sound of knocking knees!

Dress for the Show Ring
The Whip and Passengers

Unless taking part in an historical pageant or fancy dress parade, period and flowing garments should be avoided. There are a few traditional rules which it is nice to observe, such as a grey top hat for a gentleman driving his own turnout by day, but black if driving for someone else or at an evening function. Gloves are essential and brown gloves traditional even for a lady on a hot day, as pale ones will show the stain from the brown reins. They are usually leather, but string gloves are useful in wet weather.

Because of the lower level of sunlight in the British Isles, clothes of vibrant colours with large patterns that look so nice in the tropics are not traditional here. Dark blue, subtle autumn shades and heather colours have been used to great effect in the past, with perhaps a small splash of stronger colour picking out the wheel or panel of the carriage. It is the animal who should catch the eye of the spectator, with the whole turnout being in harmony. For the National and larger County Shows and events, it is correct for a gentleman driving a team, pair or tandem to wear a top hat, as he should do when driving a smart Gig to a stepping horse. At other times, correct dress is either black, brown or grey to tone with his turnout, worn with a suit or shirt (with matching collar) and tie. Black or brown shoes or jodhpur boots with non-slip soles should be worn.

For the modern exercise cart classes at small shows, a gentleman may feel overdressed wearing a bowler, in which case a country hat of the trilby variety may be preferred, or even a nice panama for a hot, bright day.

The lady Whip's outfit needs to be practical as well as feminine. Therefore a tailored dress or suit (with a little peep at cuff and collar of the pretty blouse concealed beneath the jacket) may be worn with either trousers or skirt or a divided skirt. This skirt should not be of the very tight style as this can hamper a quick dismount in an emergency. Shoes or boots with a low heel and non-slip soles will also avoid an added complication to a quick dismount, and will be firmer on the floor of the carriage whilst driving.

The subject of ladies' hats is a dangerous minefield as each lady, whether wearer or watcher, has her own strong ideas on the subject. However, hats with large brims catch the wind and are liable to blow off and are constantly having to be grasped and worried about. The shapely brim that frames the face so prettily when observed in the mirror may have a very different effect when folded back by the wind pressure! Hair should be kept neatly dressed under the hat, so that once the hat is firmly put on and adjusted it causes no more thought to the wearer.

On extremely wet show dates, tidy waterproofs are sensible, but not the shiny or highly coloured variety that are more at home in a lifeboat!

For summer wear, lightweight knee rugs are used. These are to keep the pale coloured summer clothes of the Whip and passengers clean and to preserve modesty.

On a summer-weight apron or rug, a curved corner made with perhaps a toning binding can look very smart, but a mitred corner is needed for heavier materials. If initials or monogram are to be worked onto the rug they should be of discreet size (large advertisements are for commercial use) and placed either on the outside corner or on the front near the waist.

Materials most suitable for new knee rugs and aprons are lightweight wool or linen or heavy cotton in mute colours; plain or perhaps a crossing pinstripe. Plaid should be kept for linings only.

To prevent a rug from falling, a fastening is sometimes used which allows it to be worn like an apron. This should be long enough to cover the legs and ankles when seated. When ordering or making a driving apron, careful measurements are needed so that there will be no danger of the feet becoming tangled thus causing the wearer to trip while getting in or out of the carriage. The apron should look as tidy from behind as in front. Enough material should be used to ensure a good overlap which is smooth and comfortable to sit on. This is particularly important when a waterproof fabric is being used; it is no comfort having a dry lap when sitting in a puddle!

The groom should not wear an apron or knee rug but passengers should do so.

The Groom

Traditionally, a carriage groom was male and his dress blended with the carriage, his coat being made from the same box cloth as used on the cushions, fall and lining of the folding head. His white breeches were made of buckskin and kept white with the use of a chalk block. His long black riding boots were folded down at the top showing the tan lining. This helped to keep the boot blacking off the white breeches and the whitening showing on the black. At a later date, such boots gave way to a shorter style with a light coloured top.

Cravats or stocks were the fashionable neckwear of the time, a plain white being worn by the liveried groom. A black silk top hat with a cockade worn on the left side showed that a groom's employer was a Peer of the Realm, a Churchman, a Judge or held a commission in the armed forces. A different style of cockade was reserved for Royalty. Plain brown gloves were worn.

This was also the correct attire for the employed coachman, although his livery coat had the buttons on the tail arranged differently as he had to sit in it for long periods. Livery coat buttons usually had the monogram of their employer on them, and their metal matched that of the harness and bright metalwork of the carriage.

Dress livery with tricorne hat, wig, buckled shoes, knee stockings and breeches with a frocked coat were only used with the Dress Carriage, Town Coach or Chariot on state or very formal occasions. Nowadays, this dress livery is only used by the staff of the Royal Mews and a very few others on a Royal occasion. Other than this it is relegated to the pantomime and the film industry.

The dress of the modern groom depends largely upon finance. For the show ring, the accompanying groom can be dressed as a companion; suit and bowler hat with brown gloves for a man and, for the lady companion, a practical feminine outfit which looks nice but can be worked in. Smart trousers, culottes or skirt so that she can remain dignified whatever course of action may be required of her. No driving apron, but gloves, and shoes without high or fancy heels but ideally with anti-slip soles.

For larger shows and more formal turnouts when the

groom sits on the rumble seat, livery should be worn. The livery coat should tone with the dark bodywork of the carriage and the following should be worn: black boots with tan or pale tops to them; white or light cream breeches; brown gloves; white stock; silk top hat, with the hair neatly dressed using a net if necessary (for male or female). There should be no jewellery or heavy make up. The liveried groom does not wear a buttonhole flower.

Because of the expense of turning out a liveried groom and the advent of the girl groom it has become acceptable for her to wear full hunting dress, although perhaps a shirt with a collar and tie is more in keeping than a stock as she will not be expected to ride.

When a traditional country vehicle is being driven in the show ring, a mixture of gently coloured tweed jacket and cavalry twill trousers with brown or grey bowler is nice for either sex. For the modern exercise carriage much the same dress applies with perhaps a less dressy flat cap or trilby.

When a young person acts as groom for their parents, it may be preferable for them to wear a hard riding hat, in which case, jodhpurs and jacket with shirt and Pony Club tie (if applicable), jodhpur boots and brown gloves is a neat and practical outfit.

For cross-country, a safety helmet is a sensible precaution for all on the carriage. With matching silks and sweaters in team colours it looks very workmanlike and smart.

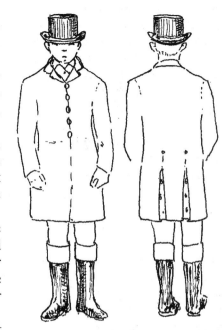

Coat with five buttons

Traditional groom's attire.

Ready-tied
Newmarket stock

Military cockade

Civil and naval cockcade

Royal cockcade

Cockade in place

Plaiting

To plait or not to plait? This is a question often asked. As a general guide for show classes, it is usual for clean-legged animals to be exhibited with plaited manes. However, the main reason for plaiting the mane is to enhance the neck of the animal for, as every woman knows, a special 'hair-do' helps celebrate a special occasion.

A nicely pulled mane and tail do credit not only to the animal but also the skilled groom who has taken the time and trouble to train the mane to lie over properly and the tail to flow out in the shape that will flatter the quarters best. However to achieve these shapes takes time and, in this age of hurry, it may not always be practically possible. Therefore plaiting may well be the answer.

On a Mountain and Moorland type of pony, the full mane and tail (along with the feather) are part of his natural beauty, so they should be left full and shown clean and free. However, a tail so long that it drags on the ground is dangerous, because it may be stepped on. This can be trimmed carefully without making a straight line, shortening it to about 2–4 cm (1–1½ in) from the ground. Very often, the forelock and mane of such ponies are so thick that it is difficult to get the bridle to fit. In this case, a carefully scissored parting or bridle path can be cut to allow the headpiece of the bridle to sit snugly and safely. Once the bridle is on, no one will see the path. One plait just behind

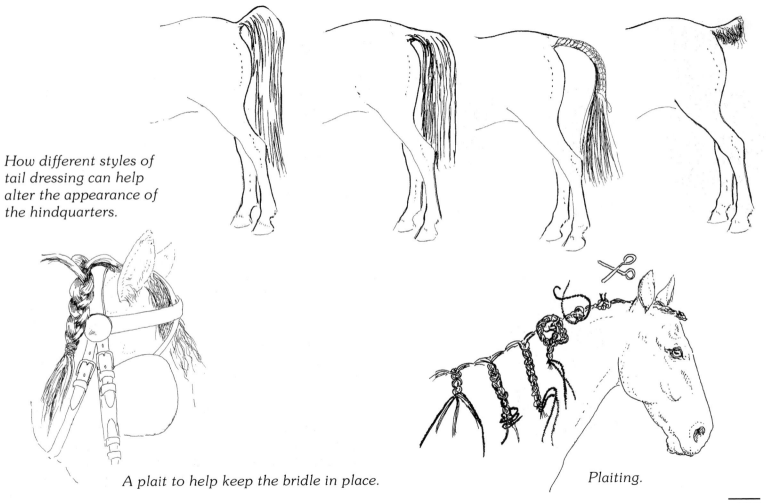

How different styles of tail dressing can help alter the appearance of the hindquarters.

A plait to help keep the bridle in place.

Plaiting.

the ears will show off a nice crest, and show how the pony's head is 'set on' the neck. This is usual with Welsh Sections A, C and D.

Once the decision to plait the mane has been taken, the style is decided by the eye of the owner and the manual dexterity of the groom. The mane will need a little tidying by pulling in the usual way, before being damped and divided into an uneven number of sections and plaited. The plaits are secured with rubber bands or stitched up into little sausage or bun shapes.

The traditional way of plaiting a coach horse was with short lengths of wool (of the same colour as the running gear of the coach). These were incorporated into each plait and used to tie the end. The plait was then twisted up and tied in a round knot and the wool used to secure it.

Plaiting the tail was not traditional for light harness horses because they suffered docking and nicking. Horses sometimes swish their tails over the rein and then clamp their docks down tight, trapping the rein and causing an accident. To prevent this, the bone was cut off (docked) leaving only about 12–20 cm (5–8 in) of dock. Sometimes the lower tendons of the tail were also severed (nicked) leaving the top ones intact; these pulled the tail upwards at a 'fashionable angle'. The hair was then allowed to grow again and cut off square, making a fan tail or cocked tail. This style can be seen depicted in many paintings by Stubbs and Aldin. These barbarous practices were outlawed by an Act of Parliament in 1949.

Although the danger from clamping the tail still exists, it is nowadays solved by humane means. A double-docked crupper is used to prevent clamping, and a tail-set crupper can be used to hold the tail up temporarily at an angle to enhance the look of the quarters.

The use of brush or comb patterns in the coat of a dri-

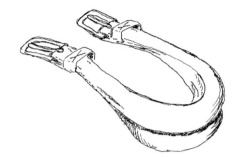

Double crupper, used to prevent tail clamping.

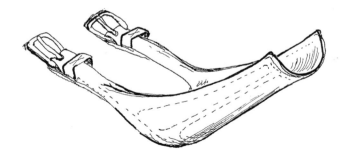

Tail set or spoon dock, used temporarily to enhance tail carriage.

ving horse is not usual because the harness interferes with them, but it may be possible to use them to draw attention to the quarters of a show horse when a false breeching is being used.

It can be a good idea to keep a tail from being clogged with mud while driving across country. This can be done either by bandaging up the tail in the same way as a polo pony's, or by plaiting it down to the end. In the latter case, either leave it one long plait, or knot it up. In order to avoid a kicking session, accustom the animal to this style at home before attempting it at a show.

In order to bulk up a thin, wispy tail, small plaits can be put in while the tail is wet. When it is dry, they are undone and carefully brushed out, and the tail will appear fuller.

Whatever choice is made regarding the animal's presentation, the reason for his having a mane and tail – protection from flies, cold and rain – should not be forgotten.

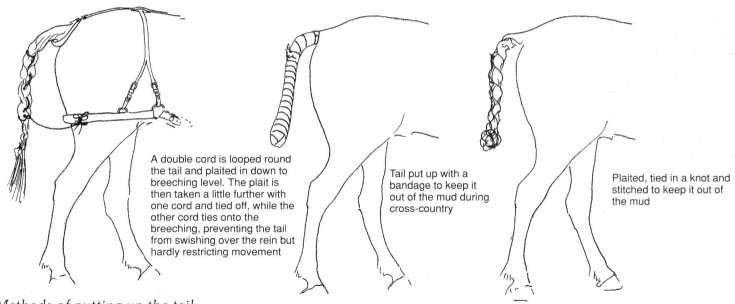

A double cord is looped round the tail and plaited in down to breeching level. The plait is then taken a little further with one cord and tied off, while the other cord ties onto the breeching, preventing the tail from swishing over the rein but hardly restricting movement

Tail put up with a bandage to keep it out of the mud during cross-country

Plaited, tied in a knot and stitched to keep it out of the mud

Methods of putting up the tail.

CHAPTER 15

Transportation

Transporting driving animals and driving vehicles from place to place, in circumstances where it is impractical for the former to pull the latter, is by no means an easy undertaking. If you intend to travel your turnout to rallies, shows and competitions, a good deal of care, preparation and, indeed, practise will be needed to ensure the prompt and safe arrival of animals, equipment and personnel. The following guidelines will, hopefully, assist you in achieving these aims.

Transporting Driving Animals

Many families own two cars so, for them, the answer is to transporting to shows, rallies etc. may be for one car to tow a trailer containing the vehicle, while the other tows the horse trailer. If you have not towed a trailer before, do practise how to reverse it. Better still, go to a caravan centre or some such establishment and take some lessons on reversing and generally manoeuvring a trailed vehicle behind a car.

If done thoughtlessly, travelling can be a very unnerving and frightening experience for any animal and especially for the equine variety, who seem to have inbuilt 'panic buttons'.

Horses, ponies and donkeys who have changed homes a lot and been through dealers' yards are usually good loaders. However, the individual family pony who has not 'travelled' can be nervous and take a long time to train. There are many methods of resolving the problems of loading and travelling and, before embarking on travelling your animal, you may wish to visit shows and rallies, to see how other people cope, and which system appeals to you. Usually, however, the following procedure will educate your animal to travel with a minimum of fuss.

If the animal has not travelled much before, or has not done so for some years, then care and patience must be exercised to teach him that there is nothing harmful inside the trailer. Well before the first outing, practise the loading programme you will be using. Fit leg and tail bandages, rugs, tail guards etc. Let the animal stand and look into the trailer where there is an inviting haynet hanging up, and maybe a bucket with some of his favourite food. Most animals will soon learn to load easily if you lead them into the trailer while telling them with a firm, calm voice to walk on. For the first time or two after tying the animal up and shutting the tailgate, just let him finish his small feed, then unload again.

If the animal will not load by leading, two people coming up from behind with a strong rope can help, the rope going round the quarters and the command 'Walk on' being quietly and firmly repeated. Usually this will work in time.

After loading and unloading at home once or twice, quietly hitch the car to the trailer. Try not to shout to other members of the family during the process, since this can upset an animal new to travelling. Move off steadily, not with a great jerk or at great speed, and drive carefully around for a short time before returning and unloading. Incidentally, it is worth every owner taking a trip in a trailer with their pony at least once to see and feel just what it is like!

Training your animal to travel happily will be a great contribution to the fun you have driving, and the practise journeys will teach him that he will always return home.

If you are in a position to have acquired a horsebox, so much the better. They always give a smoother ride and have much more room to carry harness and food than a trailer. Also, in many cases, there is room for the driving vehicle to be carried as well. Often the vehicle can be loaded in the day before travelling, so that only the animal has to go in on the day.

If you are buying your first horsebox, check the law carefully with regard to HGV licence requirements. These are rather complicated and depend upon the weight of any trailer as well as the box itself. Be sure, therefore, that any weight limitations will cover your needs, especially if you intend to travel your driving vehicle in the box.

Transporting Driving Vehicles

Moving driving vehicles from place to place without damaging them is not as easy as it might seem.

If a two-wheeled vehicle is carried in a trailer, the shafts can go over the tailboard or project forwards through holes cut in the front of the trailer. This should leave room for a pony, although perhaps not a horse. The shafts can be protected with shaft covers, tubes of canvas or vinyl, or sheets of foam rubber.

If a special trailer is to be used for the vehicle, it can have a hinged ramp. If this is to be left folded up on an open trailer, it will have lower wind resistance if covered with wire mesh rather than being solid. It is, though, a great advantage to have a covered trailer in which to keep the vehicle clean. Also, the vehicle may then be left loaded overnight, which saves valuable time on the morning of a show.

An alternative to ramps is a body which is hinged to the drawbar and which, by releasing a catch on the drawbar, can be let down at the back to ground level. This makes it rather easier to load the vehicle but it is worth, in any case, having a small hand-powered winch. Electric winches are invaluable for loading vehicles into lorries and turn this into a single-handed operation, as the shafts can be held whilst operating the winch.

Another possibility is to carry the vehicle in the back of a pickup, which also pulls the trailer containing the driving animal. This is economical, but the trailer will have to be unhitched to unload the vehicle, and the ramps will be long and rather steep.

Various other methods of transportation have been tried; carrying the vehicle on a roof-rack, dismantling it or taking off the shafts and hitching the vehicle onto the car tow hitch, but none of these has proved popular. There is, however, at least one manufacturer producing a practical vehicle which can be dismantled to fit into the back of an estate car or the front of a trailer.

Regarding methods of securing the vehicle while transporting, the usual one involves wrapping cloth or sponge rubber round the axle and then roping. The rope is how-

Transporting a driving vehicle on a trailer with movable ramp.

ever, still liable to wear through the paint and, for this reason, a section in the centre of the axle is often painted black. This, like the steps and other wear-prone points, is then easy to repaint. It is less easy to repair the damage to the wheel spokes and felloes, which often also become rubbed. The only part of a vehicle that will not be damaged by rubbing is the tyres, so if you intend to transport a vehicle regularly, it may be worth devising fixings which only make contact with the tyres. This can be done by locating one horizontal bar about 60 cm (2 ft) above the floor against the front of the wheels and another against the back of the wheels of a two-wheeler (or against the back wheels of a four-wheeler). These bars can locate into sockets on the inside walls of the trailer or horsebox, or clip onto the top edges of an open trailer. Strips of wood about 1 cm (½ in) thick should be nailed to the floor against the sides of the tyres to prevent the vehicle from bouncing sideways. If the strips are thicker than this they will rub against the tyre channels.

Securing a vehicle in transit.

CHAPTER 16

Vehicle Maintenance

Horse-drawn vehicles require maintenance to preserve their safety, performance and appearance.

Safety

Safety is the most important requirement and is mainly influenced by the condition of the wheels and axles, shafts and floor.

Wheels and Axles

Wheels should run true when picked up and spun, although 1 cm (½ in) of wobble on a wooden wheel is quite usual. However, more than this may indicate loose or rotten spokes or felloes. Check whether the felloes are bulging where the spoke enters them. If so, the felloe needs replacing, but don't be misled by the common practice of rounding off the corners of the felloe between spokes to save weight.

If the spokes are coming loose, you will see cracks in the paint where the spoke enters the stock or felloe and you may be able to twist the spoke. Check the dish of the wheel by sighting across the wheel from the felloe on one side to the other side and lining these up on the stock. The dish should be the same on each wheel. A wheel without dish is very likely to collapse under the vehicle when turning. The only exception to this is heavy artillery wheels,

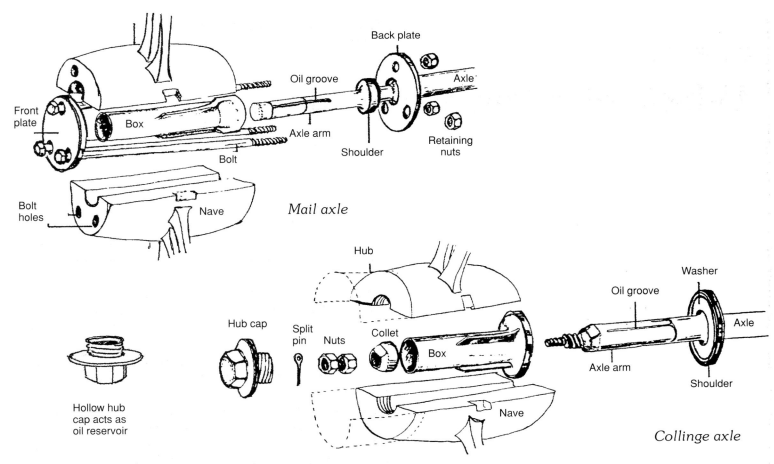

Mail axle

Front plate

Box

Bolt

Bolt holes

Nave

Oil groove

Axle arm

Shoulder

Back plate

Axle

Retaining nuts

Hollow hub cap acts as oil reservoir

Hub cap

Split pin

Nuts

Collet

Box

Hub

Nave

Oil groove

Washer

Axle

Axle arm

Shoulder

Collinge axle

Common axles and wheel bearings.

where the spokes are sandwiched between two steel washers at the stock.

In dry weather wooden wheels are prone to shrink and become loose. The first sign of this is often a creaking noise when driving. The time-honoured cure is to soak the wheels or to hang wet sacks over them, but this usually only provides a temporary cure and a 'cut and shut' by the wheelwright is soon needed.

The wheel bearings are usually either of the Mail or Collinge type. Mail axles have a collar between the wheel bearing and the spring and the wheel is held on by three bolts which pass through the stock into a steel washer trapped behind the collar. With this type of bearing, end play is taken up by leather washers either side of the collar and these should be replaced as required to reduce end play to a minimum. With a Collinge axle, there is a tapered brass collet on the outer end of the axle which mates with a taper on the end of the wheel bearing or box. This collet is adjusted and locked into place by two opposingly threaded nuts and a split pin.

Both types of axle are usually fitted with hub caps with an oil reservoir inside the hub cap. This is kept partly filled with oil and, when the vehicle is at rest, the oil lies in the lower part of the hub cap and cannot drain away. When the wheel turns, the oil is carried up onto the end of the axle and then works its way along a groove cut in the top surface. Grease should never be used in this type of bearing.

The ends of an axle slope down at the same angle as the dish of the wheel so that the lower spokes are vertical and therefore best able to carry the weight of the vehicle. You sometimes see axles which have been fitted upside down and the wheels are closer together at the top than the bottom. This is very likely to cause wheel failure, as is the more common problem where the axle has bent slightly, so that the bottom spokes are no longer vertical. There should be a very small degree of 'fore way' or 'toe in' on the wheels of a two-wheeled vehicle and the front wheels of a four-wheeler, since this helps to stop the vehicle swinging from side to side. (A more common cause of this problem with a four-wheeler driven to a single horse is the shafts being loose in the futchells.)

Most rubber tyres are now of the clencher type, but if you should be so unfortunate as to have wired tyres, you will find it very difficult to have them replaced. You may have to have the channels changed to the clencher type.

Shafts

It is essential that shafts should be sound. Should a shaft break, a two-wheeler will pitch forward. You may well be thrown forward out of the vehicle and, should you land between the vehicle and the animal with the traces still attached, perhaps with the animal starting to bolt, you would be in great danger. Shafts are most stressed slightly in front of their attachment to the front of the vehicle and

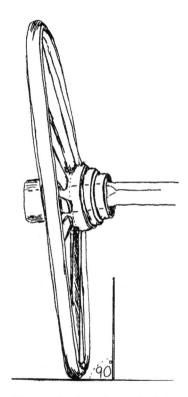

'Dish' of wheel and droop of axle keep
bottom spoke vertical

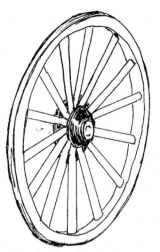

Wheel with artillery hub

Wire-on tyre

Clencher tyre

Transverse sections through tyres

Wheel details.

some carriage builders fix the shafts at this point with bolts passing through them. This weakens the shaft enormously: for instance, a vertical hole through a steel tube shaft will weaken it some ten times more than the same hole drilled horizontally.

Whatever type of shaft you have, it should be fixed to the front of the vehicle by clamps which go round the shaft. Steel shafts should not be welded at this point. The weld itself may be strong and sound but the change in stiffness is likely to cause a fatigue crack in time. The attachment at the back of the shaft is less crucial as there is much less strain here.

If the paint on wooden shafts is blistered, test the firmness of the wood with a penknife. If it is soft, replace the shafts. Vehicles should not be stored with the points of the shafts on the ground. Either use a shaft stand under the tug stops or rest the back of the vehicle on a block of wood with the shafts in the air.

Floor

The floor of a vehicle can easily be checked for soundness and for strong fastenings to the rest of the vehicle. Remember, should an animal bolt, you will be relying on a good purchase for your feet to regain control. Floors are prone to rot because the underside is often not painted as regularly as the rest of the vehicle.

Performance

Maintenance is also required to preserve the performance of the vehicle.

Tyres

If rubber tyres are allowed to wear down too far, you will find that the ride becomes progressively less comfortable. When to re-rubber wheels is a personal choice, but the deterioration in comfort will become marked when half or more of the thickness of the rubber has been worn away. Modern steel wheels with taper roller bearings do not need attention as often as the originals, but the grease will need checking every two to three years and the bearings should be kept adjusted so that the play at the wheel rim is only just detectable.

Brakes

Brakes on traditional vehicles will need replacing occasionally to extend the life of the wooden blocks, the rule being wood on rubber and rubber or leather on steel. Modern disc and drum brakes need the same maintenance as a car; bleeding the hydraulics, keeping the pistons free and replacing the pads when required. The fore carriage turntable or 'fifth wheel' needs *some* greasing, but it also needs a certain amount of friction to keep the pole steady.

Leaf Springs

The maintenance of leaf springs is problematical. If they are left alone, rust will creep out from between the leaves in wet weather and spoil the appearance. If they are taken apart and painted, the paint will soon wear off where the leaves rub together, so probably the best method is to strip and clean the springs and to put a layer of waterproof grease, of the type that used to be used for car water pumps, between the layers. The consolation is that leaf springs seem to work just as well whatever you do to them. The friction between the leaves acts as a damper and you will find that in wet weather you will get a softer but more bouncy ride.

Appearance

Maintaining the appearance of a nicely painted and varnished vehicle requires attention to several points. The greatest damage to the paint is during transport and attention to the details in the previous chapter on transport is advised. The vehicle should not be stored close to stables as the ammonia in the air will attack the paint. A dark carriage house is best, where the paint and upholstery are less likely to fade. Vehicles should be sheeted in storage, since the removal of accumulated dust and grime can scratch the varnish unless the washing is done very gently. When washing the vehicle, do not do so in strong sunlight. The water will dry too quickly, making it difficult to avoid smears, and each drop of water can act as a magnifying glass and heat the paint unevenly, which can lead to blistering.

It is usual to prepare a vehicle for show by polishing it with furniture polish. This gives a good appearance and a certain amount of protection, but has the disadvantage that all traces of the polish must be removed before the vehicle can be varnished or painted. This is especially difficult with silicone polish. Patent leather needs no treatment other than cleaning and polishing, but natural leather needs regular treatment with a product such as Ko-cho-line, to prevent it from drying out and cracking. This is especially likely to happen where the leather touches the iron framework because concealed rust will dry out the leather.

CHAPTER 17

Harness Maintenance

In the days when labour was plentiful and less expensive, the cleaning and maintenance of harness took up a good deal of the stable staff's time and energy.

For cleaning leather harness, the principles are still the same. The harness is stripped down, sweat and mud washed off with warm (not hot) water and dried off with a chamois leather. Saddle soap is rubbed into the leather work. Then, if coloured polish (black or brown as appropriate) is to be used, it is worked in with a brush to the outside and edges only.]

Next, the metal work is cleaned with a metal polish used sparingly on a piece of woollen cloth. Cotton cloth sets up a drying friction when rubbing and even more polish and elbow grease have to be used. As much attention should be paid to the back and sides of the buckles as to the fronts. The tongues of the buckles, which are of steel, will rust if careful attention is not given to them and this will also dry out the leather and cause it to crack.

If the leather work had polish put on, now is the time to buff it up with the 'off brush' and the metal work is then shone up with a soft, clean cloth. As the set of harness is reassembled it is 'finished' with a second clean, soft cloth kept for this purpose. The harness is then hung up and arranged nicely on its shaped pegs.

Many traditional harness rooms had glass-fronted cupboards to hang the harness in, as this kept the metal work from tarnishing. The bits and pole chains were made of steel and needed prompt attention after use before rusting began. They were washed off to remove the driving animals' corrosive sweat and saliva and thoroughly dried immediately. They were then cleaned with metal polish, silversand and emery cloth. Special hooks and clamps were used to hold these items firmly while they were rifted and polished. Sometimes the chains were swung vigorously in hemp sacks with silversand and polish to brighten them. The chain burnisher would then be used to restore the surface to a smooth mirror-like finish, before the chains were dusted off with a cloth which had only the slightest hint of oil on it. They were then put away in an air-tight glass-fronted cabinet.

Some harness rooms were equipped with a stout box which stood near the fire and was filled with a mixture of lime, chalk and sawdust, to bury the cleaned bit and chains in when they were not in everyday use. Perhaps this was the origin of the lucky dip bran tub game. Nowadays, we have the luxury of stainless steel, nickel and chrome, which only require to be washed, dried and polished off.

Whatever synthetic materials are used nowadays in making harness, it will still need to be cleaned (for the animal's benefit if not for the owners pride) and checked for wear and tear. When harness is purchased new the manufacturer's advice on how it should be cleaned comes with it. The usual ways are wiping off with clean soapy water, or putting through the washing machine (in a pillow case for the benefit of the machine) or brushing off with a stiff bristle brush when dry. Whichever method is decided upon, a safely fixed hanging hook is essential for ease of the cleaning and polishing process. Laying straps on a table or work bench wears out the sponges and brushes as the table surface itself is polished and soaped, and the underside and sides of the straps are either neglected, or the process has to be done twice.

The harness cleaner must be prepared to get dirty hands, as kitchen gloves wear out quickly and do not give the same feel, although they are essential if beautiful hands and nails are to be preserved. Saddle soap is also good for the hands and, if the harness is soaped before the metal polish is used, this will help to protect the finger tips from the drying effect of the metal polish. After a harness-cleaning session a thorough hand wash and nail scrubbing will be needed, along with plenty of hand cream.

When packing harness away for some time – perhaps for the winter months when it will not be used – an oily harness dressing can be rubbed into the underside, with a good smear on the tongues of the buckles. This will ensure that soft, uncorroded harness is unpacked in the spring. The box must be rodent-proof and stored in a dry but not warm place.

For travelling show or presentation harness, some kind of lightweight rigid container is needed with plenty of soft packing inside to keep the harness firm and prevent it rubbing on either itself or the box. Clingfilm or similar pressed around the bright metal work will keep it from tarnishing in transit. This is better than newspaper which shifts and blows away.

CHAPTER 18

Avoiding Accidents

Driving can be a dangerous sport and we hope that the information in this book will help keep you safe and minimise the possibility of an accident. However, before concluding, we should stress the need to take due care at all times. The basic factors which should be considered in the interests of safety are obedience to the Highway Code, consideration for others and adherence to correct driving practices.

The Highway Code

Guidance given in the Highway Code changes from time to time, and your knowledge of it should be continually updated. When driving a horse-drawn vehicle on the public highway, certain principles should be observed, especially with regard to signalling. When you are being followed by a rider or another horse-drawn vehicle, whip signals should be used, but when signalling to other road users the ruling since the late 1980s is that hand signals should be used. This means transferring the whip from your right hand to under your left thumb and using the right hand to signal to those behind having, of course, checked that the reins are balanced in your left hand and that you are in full control.

When turning right always remember to check behind, signal and then check behind again to make sure that it is quite safe to proceed. When turning left, if you have a passenger, ask them to check and signal while you, the Whip, do the final check. (It is worth remembering that, whenever possible, you should have a passenger with you. After some accidents, insurance companies have been reluctant to pay up, claiming that it is irresponsible to drive an animal without a second person present.)

Horse-drawn vehicles are not allowed on motorways, and many 'A' roads are unsuitable. The volume and type of traffic and the lack of thought and knowledge of those using combustion-engined vehicles make them really dangerous. In many cases, people nowadays do not understand the nature of horses and ponies. Therefore, when carriage driving on the highway, it is advisable to wear the traditional safety vests with their various caution warnings.

Consideration for Others

Until the late 1980s, equines – especially carriage driven animals – still had right of way on the roads. This is no longer the case and, as previously mentioned, it is now more essential than ever to treat other road users courteously. Two specific and especially relevant examples of this are given below.

Although we have the *right* to drive on the public highway at any time, considerate timing of our driving will be appreciated by other road users. They may be in a hurry to get to work on time, or to get their children to school, and a dangerous situation may be provoked which could have been avoided had we waited half an hour.

To avoid causing an accident when meeting ridden animals who may not be used to what they consider an alarming sight – a horse with wheels – be prepared to stop and get your groom down to your animal's head, and wait quietly while the riders deal with their predicament.

Correct Driving Practice

If the right harness and carriage have been chosen for the purpose required, and they are maintained to the highest standard, the harness properly fitted and the carriage balanced and put to an animal who is confident, of good temperament and well schooled, the chance of a mishap is greatly reduced. This chance can be further reduced by acting sensibly yourself, and you should also voice your fears if you feel that someone in charge of another turnout is acting in a foolhardy way. It is possible to act responsibly to protect others without being 'an interfering busybody'.

In the wild, horses use speed as their defence, running away quickly from anything they fear. Since this is their instinctive reaction, it is what happens if something they do not understand occurs. Driving animals are trained to go in a winkered bridle; they can trust the driver's hands, hear his voice and accept the feel of the vehicle. When these things change suddenly, the likelihood of an accident is greatly increased. However carefully a bridle is removed while an animal is put to, its removal will allow him to see the carriage moving close behind him, and he will run from it. A frightened, bolting horse or pony is always terrifying but, when one has a carriage attached to him, things are many times worse. As the carriage breaks up, bits of metal and splintered wood add to the dangers of injury to both the animal and anyone who cannot get out of the way. Therefore, it should be made an absolutely unbreakable rule that you always take the animal out of the vehicle and move him away before removing any part of the harness.

While the animal is being put to, the groom must not let go, nor allow him to graze. If a rein is caught under a hoof, shaft or pole, the bridle is likely to be pulled off. Also, if the animal is tied up when put to, the bridle may be dragged off by the headcollar rope.

A groom holding an animal by the bar connecting the long cheekpieces on a Buxton bit can cause trouble. If an animal suddenly throws his head up, the pressure put on his mouth will cause pain, promoting a sequence of dangers, one of which being the possible dislocation of the groom's shoulder!

One of the advantages of having a groom on the ground at halt, standing to the front of the turnout, is that there is an additional lookout so that any potential problem approaching from behind can be spotted early and dealt

Even though they may be obedient, some animals persist in looking about while standing still. The movement of the animal's head may result in a rein becoming caught under a shaft. To prevent this from happening, a rolled leather line can be clipped to tiny rings set onto the points of the shafts.

with before it becomes a disaster.

The Whip must always mount with the reins in hand so that full control is achieved at all times. Never allow a passenger to board a carriage unless the Whip is established on the box seat. At driving trials, it is not unusual to see horses running away with the referee sitting helplessly on the vehicle, while the reins trail away to one side; the Whip having been tipped out, taking the reins with him. Of course, these people have gone deliberately into a hazardous situation, somewhat different from the normal run of pleasure driving, but there are still lessons to be learnt from this predicament.

A comfortable height of cushion and amount of leg room are important to provide a strong driving position. A cushion or seat that is not firmly fixed can slide, taking the Whip with it. Some modern carriages use locker space under the box seat to carry spares. Access to this locker is gained by tipping the whole seat forwards so, if this is not securely locked, a groom grasping the back rail while getting up or down can release the whole seat and shoot the Whip over the dashboard!

Training a driving animal to go forward faster from a tongue-clicking sound is another recipe for disaster, because any bystander can take charge of him by clicking. Cracking the whip is also to be avoided, or else the sound of a breaking twig as you drive through a wood may send you surging quickly homeward. Sensible word commands delivered in an encouraging, soothing or disapproving tone come naturally to a Whip and are consistent, effective and safe.

If you do have the misfortune to have an animal bolt with you, it is generally the stopping, rather than the steering which is the problem. Stay with it and keep a cool head; steer round obstacles. If there is a safe opportunity to encourage the animals to run, this is worth doing; they sometimes stop out of surprise, or run out of steam, particularly if pointed uphill. Failing that, steer towards an object which is definitely unjumpable. When schooling a driving animal, a short canter uphill away from home will allow him to feel the different motion of the carriage which, of itself, can cause a fright if he is not used to it.

Always have your animal under such control that you consider one stride out of the speed you have chosen a runaway because, by the third stride, it will be! As stressed previously, the skill of driving lies in dealing with the situation before it arises.

First Aid

Although you should take every precaution to avoid an accident, it is also wise to take precautions which will help you to deal with one if it should arise. Therefore, the spares box should always contain a few essentials for first aid treatment of both humans and equines.

Of course, first aid treatment may be required in

circumstances less serious than accidents, for instance antiseptic cream may be needed to deal with an insect bite, or an arm or neck struck by the driving whip. In hot weather, it is always a wise precaution to have an anti-histamine spray in the spares box, as well as a fly repellent lotion for the animal (who should also have had some put on him before the outing).

The spares box should also contain one or two slings and a couple of good bandages (which can be used as tourniquets if necessary), some antiseptic lint and a small container of wound powder. Antiseptic cream without anti-histamine is useful for putting on 'broken knees' (torn skin at the knees) should your animal be unfortunate enough to stumble and damage them. The cream will help keep the knees clean until you reach home and will prevent the injuries from becoming dry and crusty. Incidentally, a sound, old-fashioned way of dealing with 'broken knees' is to hose the wounds for a few minutes two or three times a day until they really start to heal, and to keep them open to the air. It is amazing how quickly healing occurs with this treatment.

If, by some dreadful bad luck, you and your turnout are involved in an accident, remember the following:

Always stay with your vehicle until the moment of impact, saying 'Steady' or 'Whoa' in the calmest voice you can manage; this may slow things down and minimise the effect of impact.

If your animal ends up on the ground, keep repeating the command 'Stand'. This sometimes works to keep a well trained animal still and, if it does, a lot of further complications may be avoided. In such a situation, it is often best to remove such harness as is necessary to allow the vehicle to be pulled away while the animal is still down and then, if no limbs are broken, to long-rein him upright. Dress any cuts and grazes with wound powder. If there are any more serious injuries, send for the nearest vet, but be prepared to apply a tourniquet if necessary.

If a person has been thrown out of the vehicle and is lying unconscious, remember that they may have hit their head on something hard, so do not try to move them. Put a coat, or even a sweat rug over them, and call an ambulance.

We would suggest that all Whips learn basic first aid for both people and driving animals.

CHAPTER 19

Additional Animals

We have mentioned, in passing, that most types of equine can, and have been driven in harness and, in other times and places, various other animals – including oxen and llamas – have been used in draught. In the hope that all readers will derive as much fun and pleasure from the association with the animals as from the driving itself, let us draw your attention to two other creatures associated with the 'fun' aspect.

The Goat in Harness

The goat can be useful as a draught animal; although small he is very strong. He is however, unable to take his place in serious driving because he can only work for short periods before needing to lie down and chew the cud! There are many early photographs of harnessed goats giving pleasure to children, and being used as a novelty on the sea fronts. They conveniently sat down between the shafts while not being driven and, being such individual characters, probably also while they *were* driven!

Tiny sets of goat harness with open-top collars can still be found. They are often very decoratively embossed with shell-shaped blinkers, or piped with coloured patent leather. Miniature carriages of all types were built to the highest of standards. Nowadays, both harness and carriages have to be made specially for goats. The same measuring points are used as those advised earlier for horses

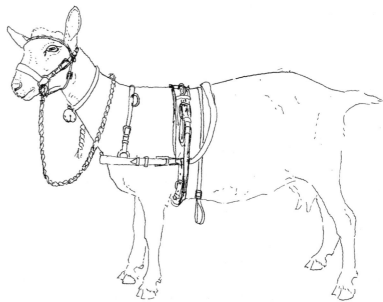

Goat harness was often elaborately embossed. With the goat's short, flexible tail, a crupper was not used, the breeching being held in place with a loin strap behind the hip bones. Goats were driven from either a bit or noseband.

Modern goat harness is often made of webbing, using an open headcollar-type bridle and false breeching.

and ponies.

The principles of harnessing, putting to and balance are the same as for equines. Very thin bits can be used in their mouths, but reins can also be fastened to the nose-band with great effect. A goat learns what is required of him rather in the same way as a dog learns; through being led about, with plenty of voice commands and rewards.

If the goat is to be driven on the road, a bell should be hung around his neck and another fixed to the harness in order to comply with the law that an unshod animal should have some audible sign of approach.

For those who enjoy the unusual, sheep also make an interesting draught animal.

The Coaching Dog – The Dalmatian

The origins of the once seen, never forgotten breed, the Dalmatian, are clouded in mystery. In England, as the wheel of history turns, we find the spotted dog running close to it.

When freight was carried by long trains of pack horses, a strong, familiar figure was on guard. In the Regency period, the carriage dog was not just a fashionable accoutrement and ornament to the turnout, but a practical working dog. He was a strong dog with a good shoulder and compact feet, built to trot all day beside the master's carriage. At night, he would lie under the vehicle in the yard of some strange inn, his dark spots breaking up his shape in the shadows. A thief up to no good would be attacked silently and unseen. The coachman of yesteryear chose a white-faced dog with dark ears, eyes and muzzle, so his head would resemble a skull. This was enough to scare anyone away!

Nowadays, in the dog show ring, a bald-faced dog is frowned upon. The modern carriage enthusiast looking for a dog to complete their turnout should go to a reputable breeder. You should choose a big, strong puppy, who comes out from the litter to greet you. Check that he is not deaf, that he has compact feet, a well-pigmented nose and dark rims to his brown eyes. Choose a nice, old-fashioned coaching name to give him. There is a host of coach builders and coachmen of yesteryear who had wonderful sounding names; Dennett, Ward, Tilbury, Selby, Truett, Beaufort and Lawton are just a few.

Dalmatians grow large and boisterous and can be difficult to train. Be firm but kind. A local obedience training class is a great help with the initial training. As with children, your adult dog is what you have made him. With a bit of luck he will be with you for about twelve years, so he is worth initial time and trouble.

Most Dalmatians have inherent instincts to run under the axle, but some have not. Start the training with ordinary heel work on and off the lead, then follow the vehicle yourself getting closer and closer. At heel, your dog will gain his confidence from you. A four-wheeler with a hind step at the side is ideal for training because you can stand on this as the vehicle moves along. The dog will thus gain confidence, and you will not be worn out by running. Any centre step should be temporarily removed beforehand so that he will not hurt himself while learning to run under.

While training, you may need to tie the dog to prevent him from going too far forward. He must be secured only with a quick-release knot and be accompanied by someone whose sole job is to free him. Your dog will probably learn to respect the wheels the hard way, so encourage him to be under while moving the vehicle around by hand. You may be able to knock him with the wheel, thus saving a pinched paw or worse later on.

If a bell is attached to the dog's collar it can be heard ringing as he trots, and you can hear whether he is under the axle or has gone off rabbiting! With the modern speed and volume of traffic, a careful choice of driving routes will have to be made so that there is no danger for the dog from traffic.

Dalmatians are great family dogs, who usually guard well and love to accompany you whenever you go driving in the car or out with the carriage. The only drawback is that they moult permanently, so white hairs will always be a feature of your clothes. Also, they are great dustbin explorers, but once you have owned one, you will never want to be without your 'Dally'.

So, finally, happy driving . . . . .and goodbye!

Index

Page numbers in *italics* refer to illustrations

accident avoidance 164–8
aprons 35, 145–6
Arabs 13
articulation in tandem driving 120, 121–2
axles 49, 53, 156, *157*, 158, *159*

back band 54, 57, 69–70, *75*, 78
back strap 69–70
balance strap 109
bearing rein 28, 80, *81*
belly band 76, 77, 78, 79
bit 28, *59*, 60, *74*, 87
   goat 171
   single harness 72, 73, *74*
blinkers 28, 73, *75*
Body Break 51, 94
bolting 165, 166, 167
box seat *90*
brakes 50, 160–1
breeching 70, *71*, 72, *75*, 77, 78, 79
   donkey 80
   false 76
   pair harness 98
   strap 76, 78
bridle 28–9, 79
   donkey 80

single harness 72–3, *74*, *75*
   tandem driving 113
bridoon *81*
British Driving Society 2, 3, 6, 83
broken knees 168
Broughams 137
brushing boots, temporary *38*
bugle bar *105*, *106*, 107
Butcher's Cart 135

Cabriolet 41
Cape harness 107, *108*, 109
carriage 129
   builders 43–4, 171
   team driving 125
changing rein 142
Charabancs 125
coat 24–5
cockade 146, *148*
Cocking Carts 113
collar 54, 60, *61*, 62–4, 79
   donkey 80
   fit 60, 62–4
   full 60, 66, *68*
   measuring for 62
   pair harness 94, *95*
   single harness 65–6, *67–8*, 69
   tandem harness 117
   team harness 126
   and traces 31

collar, breast 60, *63*, 64, 65, *66*, *67*, 79
   pair harness *96*
   swingle tree 49, *50*, 77
collecting ring 141
Collinge axle *157*, 158
colour 93–4, 134
comb patterns 150–1
combined driving 6–7
competitive driving 5–7
cones 7, 122
Connemara ponies 13, *14*
coupling buckle 100, *101*, 102
coupling strap 126
crupper 69–70, *75*, 79
   dock 57, 70, *75*, 79, 117
   double-docked 150
   tail-set 150
curb chain 87
Curricle 103, *104*, 107
   Cape 107, *108*, 109
   harness 103, *105–6*
   putting to 103, 107

Dales ponies 13, *17*
Dalmation dog 171–2
Dartmoor ponies 13, *16*
Demi Tonneau 51, *52*
disabled people 8–9
dishing 21
dismounting 84–5

docking 150
Dog Cart 51, *52*, 94
dogs, coaching 171–2
donkeys 12–13, 80, 109
drag shoe 129
draghout 109
dress 35
   show ring 144–7, *148*
dressage 6
driving
   art 85–9
   clubs 1–2
   correct practice 165–7
   cross-country *97*
   emergency stops 87–8, 121
   from the vehicle 32–3
   long distance 2, 6
   machine 89, 126, 129
   non-competitive 2–5
   off-vehicle practise 89
   position *90*, 91, *92*, *138*, 167
   preparation 83–5
   technique changes 82–3
   use of hands 85–7
   whip use 88–9
driving animal 10–22
   breeds 13
   care 23–6
   conformation 18, *19–20*, 21–2
   cost 12

   feeding 25–6
   matching 12
   movement 18, 21–2
   size 11–12
   specific uses 12
   temperament 13, 18
   training to harness 27–33
   transportation 152–3
   vehicle size *45*

emergency stops 87–8, 121
Equirotal Carriage 50, *51*
exercise 24, 25
Exmoor ponies 13, *16*
eye 18

Fell ponies 13, *15*
fetes 4
first aid 167–8
fitness 23–5
Flatbed Carts *136*, 137
Float 53
fly protection 5, 151
forging 21
four-in-hand driving 2, 126, 129
four-wheeler, harness 94

gait change 102
galling 25
Gelderlanders *17*, 94

Gig 51, *52*, 55
girth 77, 79
    Curricle 103, *105*
    false 109, *127*
gloves 144
goats 169, *170*, 171
Governess Cart 47, 51, *52*, 53
grass 25
groom 40–1, 83, 166–7
    dress 146–7, *148*
    show ring 142–3
    team driving 129
grooming 25, 148, *149*, 150–1

Hackneys 13, *15*, 80, 94
hame strap 66
hames 60, 62, 63, 79
    fitting 66, *68*
    tandem driving 117
    team harness *127*
handbrake 129
hands 85–7
Hansom Cab *46*, 47
hard food 25
harness 4, 7, 25
    choice 54, *55–6*, 57, *58–9*, 60, *61*, 62–4
    cost 12
    donkeys 80
    four-wheel vehicle 79, 94

Gig 55
goat 169, *170*, 171
    maintenance 162–3
    measuring for *55*
    mules 80
    pair vehicles 94, *95–7*, *105-6*, 107, *108*, 109
    Park Drag *132*
    Repairs 38
    Road Coach *132*
    storage 163
    tandem 113, *114–15*, 117
    team driving 125–6, *127*
    trade *134*
    see also collar; crupper; pad; saddle; trace; tug
harness, single
    back band 69–70
    back strap 69–70
    bit 72, 73, 74
    breeching 70, *71*, 72
    bridle 72–3, *74*, *75*
    collar 65–6, *67–8*, 69
    crupper 69–70
    driving 82–9, *90*, *91*, *92*
    false martingale 69
    fitting 65–6, *67–8*, 69–70, *71*, 72–3, *74–5*
    pad 69–70
    pairs 94

    putting to 77–8
    reins 72, 73
    saddle 69–70
    taking out 78–7
    traces 69
    tugs 69–70
    variations 79–80, *81*
harnessing
    driving pairs 98
    tandem driving 117–19
hats 144, 145, 146
hay 26
headcollar 78
Highland ponies 13, *14*
Highway Code 164–5
horsebox 153
horsemanship 140
hub caps 158

individual display 143
insect bites 5, 168
insurance 4, 165

Jaunting Car 51, *52*

knee rugs 35, 145, 146

lamps 131, *133*
leaf springs 161
legs 18, *20*, 21–2

Leicester Car 51, *52*
line of draught 63, *64*
Liverpool bit 28, *59*, *74*, *75*
livery 146, 147
loading 152–3
long-reining 24, 28, 29
lungeing 24, 29

Mail axle *157*, 158
mane 148, *149*, 150
marathon 6–7
martingale
   Cape harness 109
   false 64, 69, *75*
Milk Float 135
mounting 84, 167
moving off 32, 100
mule harness 80
musical drive 4

New Forest ponies *17*

overtracking 22

pad *56*, *75*, 79
   Curricle *107*
   donkey 80
   pair harness 94
   single harness 69–70
pair driving 12, 93–4, *95–7*,

98–100, *101*, 102
   colour 93–4
   costs 93, 94
   gait change 102
   harnessing up 98
   moving off 100
   problems 102
   putting to 99
   rein handling 100
   in step 102
   swing pair *98*
   taking out 99
   vehicles 103, *104*, 107
pair harness 94, *95–7*, *105–6*, 107, *108*, 109
   breeching 98
   coupling reins 99, 100, *101*, 102
   pole straps 99
   traces 99, 100
Park Drag
   harness *132*
   horse colour 134
   show ring 130–1, *132*
passengers 165
Phaeton 51, *52*, 125
pickaxe team *128*
picnics 4–5
plaiting 21, 148, *149*, 150–1
pole
   Cape Curricle 107, 109

chains/straps 94, *95*, *97*, 98, 99, 103
   Curricle 103, *106*
   head, hook and crab *127*
pony teams 125
private driving 137
pulling 102
   tyre, log or harrow 31
putting to 76–8, 166
   Cape harness 109
   Curricle 103, 107
   driving pairs 99
   first time 31–2
   preparing 76
   tandem driving 119–23

quarters 18, 22

Ralli Car 51, 94
rallies 3
reflective material 39
reins 75, 79, 87
   attachments for driving bits *74*
   coupling 99, 100, *101*, 102
   draught 100
   holding 83, 85, *86*, 87
   pair harness 94, 100
   repairs *38*
   scurry driving 7
   single harness 72,73

tandem driving 111, *116*, 117–8, 119–21
team driving 126, *128*
Riding for the Disabled Association 8
Road Coach 126, 134
    hames *127*
    harness *132*
    show ring 131, *132*, 134
road use 83, 165
roger ring 113, *114*, *115*

saddle *56*, 69–70, *75*
safety 4, 5
    checks 83
    helmet 147
    roads 83
    vehicle 156, 158, 160
    vests 33, 165
schooling 21
    professional 27–8
scurry driving 7, 91
shafts 45, *48*, 76, 78, 158, 160
    flexibility 46, 47
    four-wheel vehicle 79
    independent 79
    materials 47
    springing *48*
Shetland ponies *11*, 13, *15*
shoeing 24
shopping 5

show ring *132–3*, 134–5, *136*, 137, *138*, 139–48, *149*, 150–1
    changing rein 142
    collecting ring 141
    dress 144–7, *148*
    entering 141-2
    individual display 143
    judge 137, 142, 143, 144
    line-ups 142–4
    manners 142
    Park Drag 130-1, *132*
    plaiting 148, *149*, 150–1
    private driving 137
    propriety 144
    Road Coach 131, *132*, 134
    spectating 130
    technique 139–44
    trade class 134-5, *136*, 137
    vehicle preparation 161
skid pan 129, 134
sores 25
spares kit 37–9, 168
speed 3, 12
splinter bar 49
spoon dock *150*
stock 146, *147*
straps, breaking 38
swing pair *98*
swingle tree 49, *50*, 77, *98*, *127*

tail 148, *149*, 150–1
tandem
    bars *114*, *115*, 119, 123
    sporting *112*
Tandem Carts 113
tandem driving 2, 110–11, *112*, 113, *114–16*, 117–23
    articulation 120, 121–2
    cones 122
    emergency stop 121
    English style 119–21
    harness 113, *114–15*, 117
    Hungarian style 119, 121–2
    lead traces 123
    leader 117–18, 122, 123
    line of draught *116*
    problems 122–3
    putting to 118–19
    reins 111, *116*, 117–18, 119–21
    techniques 119–23
    vehicle 111, *112*, 113
    wheeler 117, 118, 122, 123
team driving 124–6, *127–8*, 129
    handbrake 129
    harness 125–6, *127*
    leaders 129
    moving off 129
    pickaxe *128*
    reins 126, *128*
    unicorn *128*

vehicle 129
  wheelers 129
teeth 23
terret 72, *75*
  Curricle 103, *105*, *106*
  tandem harness *114*, *116*, 117, *118*
  team harness *127*
Thoroughbreds 13
Tiger 41, 103
trace *75*, 76–7, 79
  carrier *64*
  ends 57, *58*
  pair harness 94, 99, 100
  tandem harness 117, 118–19, 123
  team driving 126
trace hooks 57, *58*, 60, 76, 77
  spring 49, *50*
trade class 134–5, *136*, 137
trailer 153
training at home 28–9, 30, 31–3
transport 4
transportation 152–5
  driving animals 152–3
  driving vehicles 154–5
treasure hunts 3
tug 57, 63, 69–70, *75*, 76, 78
  buckle 117, *127*
  team harness *127*
  Tilbury 79

turnout 4
tyres
  pneumatic 53
  rubber 158, *159*, 160

unfitness signs 24
unharnessing 78–9, 166
unicorn team 128

vehicle 4
  appearance 161
  balance 45–7, 77–8, 83
  body 49
  cab-fronted 53
  choice 42–4, *48*, 49–51, *52*, 53
  compatible animal *139*, *140*, *141*
  competition 50–1
  disabled drivers 8, *9*
  dismounting 84–5
  floor 160
  four-wheel 53, 113
  leaf springs 161
  maintenance 156, *157*, 158, *159*, 160–1
  mounting 84
  performance 160–1
  safety 156, 158, 160
  tandem driving 111
  team driving 125
  transportation 154–5

two-wheel 53, 113
types 51, *52*, 53
  see also axles; brakes; shafts; tyres; wheels
voice aids 28, 29, 88, 100, 168

Waggonette 51, *52*, 94, 125
walking 85
water 26
waterproofs 145
weddings 4
Welsh ponies 13, *15*, *16*, *17*, 150
wheelchairs 8–9
wheels 49, 50–1, 156, 158, *159*
  bearings *157*, 158
  dish 49, 156, *159*
  hub 158, *159*
whip 35–6
  cracking 167
  holding 84, 87
  signals 164
  use 88–9
Whip
  disabled 8
  dress 4, 6, 7, 137
  show ring dress 144–6
  style 137
Wilson snaffle 60, *74*
winker *see* blinker
worming 23